WORD
DROPS

PAUL ANTHONY JONES

WORD DROPS

A SPRINKLING OF LINGUISTIC CURIOSITIES

First published 2015 by
Elliott and Thompson Limited
27 John Street
London WC1N 2BX
www.eandtbooks.com

ISBN: 978-1-78396-153-5

9 8 7 6 5 4 3 2

A catalogue record for this book is available from the British Library.

Typesetting: Marie Doherty

Printed in the UK by TJ International Ltd.

For Matthew and Anthony

Introduction

Tucked away alongside entries like *logogram*, *logodaedalus* ('one who is cunning in words') and the considerably less pleasant but no less evocative *logodiarrhoea* ('a flux or flow or words'), the *Oxford English Dictionary* includes a brief entry dedicated to *logofascinated* – an adjective, it explains, meaning 'fascinated by words'. Only one record of its use in print is provided, taken from a relatively little-known work by the Scottish author and translator Sir Thomas Urquhart dating from 1652. As a noted *logodaedalus* Urquhart himself presumably coined the word, in which case he probably intended it to bear out the original and now long-lost seventeenth-century meaning of *fascinated* as a synonym of 'bewitched' or 'enchanted'. If you're *logofascinated*, ultimately, you're literally 'spellbound' by language.

Whatever its history and connotations may be, however – and despite its criminally infrequent use in print – there is little denying that *logofascinated* is an absolutely superb word. It neatly sums up that inherent curiosity with words and language that leads to much eyebrow-raising and appreciative head-tilting whenever we stumble upon some new or remarkable word, or learn of some bizarre etymological quirk or tall tale. My own 'logofascination' began as an eight-year-old, when I was given a fine-looking hardback dictionary for Christmas by my grandparents; by Boxing Day afternoon I had read it cover to cover, diligently devouring every page and dutifully taking note of any unfamiliar words encountered en route. Now, I openly admit that reading a dictionary cover to cover might not be everyone's idea of a Christmas (or indeed any day) well spent – and in retrospect, that level of nerdishly obsessive logofascination probably outsteps even Urquhart's original definition – but I can be consoled by the fact that, as a lover of language, I am by no means alone.

Two decades later, in December 2013, I set up a Twitter account called @HaggardHawks, through which I began tweeting word and language facts, strange and surprising etymologies, unusual and archaic words, and a daily Word of the Day pulled from one of the quirkier, dustier corners of the dictionary. Within a week, my handful of curious first followers had unexpectedly been joined by another hundred Twitterers who, like me, shared a common interest in the idiosyncrasies of our language. Within a month, that number had grown tenfold. Going into the New Year, *Haggard Hawks* – so-called, I should point out, as *haggard* was originally a falconer's term describing a wild hawk – was profiled in *The Huffington Post*, named as one of Twitter's best language accounts by *Mental_Floss* magazine, and added its 5,000th follower in the summer of 2014. As it continued to grow, *Haggard Hawks* soon established itself as a whole new project in its own right, demanding almost as much original research and organisation as the books I had previously written. But it seemed a shame to leave all this wonderful linguistic trivia in the electronic ether, and so a plan emerged to cherry-pick some of the best facts from its first semester and set them down in print; the book you now hold in your hands is ultimately the handsome offspring of @HaggardHawks.*

---

* Twitter lends itself brilliantly to trivia: the 140-character limit keeps facts brief yet digestible, succinct but no less informative. It can sometimes be just as frustrating, however, as some of the more intriguing words and trivia are obliged to stand alone while their equally fascinating back stories and explanations are left unsaid. Here in print though, this can be redressed: additional notes have been added throughout the book to fill in these blanks, providing welcome context, clarification and anecdotal evidence to bolster the bare facts.

In compiling these early bare bones of *Word Drops*, however, it soon became apparent that clutches of tweeted trivia seemed somehow to work – or rather 'drop' – together. The fact that, for instance, the *Jerusalem* of 'Jerusalem artichoke' is actually *girasole*, the Italian word for 'sunflower', appeared to sit perfectly beside the old French idiom *avoir un cœur d'artichaut*, 'to have a heart like an artichoke', which describes someone who seems fickly to fall in love with everyone they meet. And speaking of artichokes, in Scots they were once nicknamed *worry-baldies*, which tied in nicely with *phalacrophobia*, the fear of going bald. In turn, *phalacrophobia* derives from the same root as *phalacrocorax*, the Latin name for the cormorant, which literally means 'bald raven'. And a group of cormorants is called a *gulp*, incidentally, which also means 'to swallow noisily' – as do *slonk*, *frample* and *gamf*. But the opposite of all of those is probably *fletcherisation*, which means 'chewing your food at least thirty times before swallowing'. I'll stop there (you can see how that continues on page 168), but it was from word association chains just like these that *Word Drops* was born.

Before we begin – in the only place it would really be right to – let me take the opportunity to quickly but sincerely give thanks to all the followers of @HaggardHawks, without whom this project would likely never have come about. Thanks also to my agent, Andrew Lownie; to Jennie Condell, Pippa Crane and all at Elliott & Thompson; to my parents and expert proofreaders Leon and Maureen Jones; and to all of the centuries-spanning authors of the dictionaries and glossaries from which many of the most unlikely and unfamiliar of words listed here have been taken – a select list of their wonderful works is provided here for reference.

Paul Anthony Jones
November 2014

Aardvark means 'earth-pig' in Afrikaans.

[The aardvark is a peculiar African mammal whose equally peculiar double-A name has earned it its prestigious position as the first animal in the dictionary. Spare a thought, then, for its alphabetical next-door neighbours, the *aardwolf* and *aasvogel*, who are pipped into second and third place: the aardwolf (literally the 'earth-wolf') is a small striped hyena that's also known as the *maanhaar*, as if one set of double As wasn't enough, while the aasvogel (or 'carrion-bird') is another name for the Cape vulture, one of Africa's largest birds of prey. All three creatures take their names from Afrikaans, a South African language that developed from Dutch in the early 1700s.]

♦

The Italian equivalent of 'when pigs fly' is *quando voleranno gli asini* – or 'when donkeys fly'.

♦

A cross between a female donkey and a male zebra is called a *zedonk*.

♦

Hippotigrine means 'zebra-like' or 'zebra-striped'.

♦

An Old Testament description of a hippopotamus is thought to be the origin of the word *behemoth*.

[*Behemoth* derives from the Hebrew *b'hemoth*, which appears in the Book of Job 40:15–24 as the name of an enormous creature with 'bones ... as strong as pieces of brass' that 'moveth his tail like a cedar'. Job's description is so ambiguous that the true identity of his *behemoth* remains a mystery, and in the past suggestions have ranged from an elephant to a water buffalo to a crocodile to (among some Young Earth Creationists, at least) a gigantic dinosaur. But given that we are told that the behemoth, 'lieth under the shady trees, in the covert of the reed and fens', where 'he eateth grass as an ox', and 'can draw up [the river] Jordan into his mouth', the most likely explanation is that he's a hippopotamus.]

♦

Hippocampus is the Greek word for 'seahorse'.

[All mammalian brains contain two seahorse-shaped *hippocampi* (although some early anatomists thought they looked more like silk-worms) that together play a part in various mental faculties like spatial awareness, memory and emotional response. *Hippocampus* is actually a compound of the Greek words for 'horse' (*hippos*) and 'sea-monster' (*kampos*), and was originally the name of a literal 'sea-horse' depicted in ancient artworks as a monstrous hybrid of a horse and a dolphin.]

♦

Male seahorses are nicknamed *sea-stallions*.

♦

Walrus means 'whale-horse'.

♦

Igunaujannguaq, or 'frozen walrus carcass', is a traditional Inuit game in which someone trying to remain as still as possible is handed from player to player.

[Suggesting a round of 'frozen walrus carcass' might not sound like the best way to wile away a lazy afternoon, but *igunaujannguaq* is nevertheless a popular game amongst the Nunavut Inuit of Canada.

What few rules there are demand that the player acting as the 'walrus' should remain as stiff as possible (preferably with his or her feet fixed in place by those of a circle of players, so that they can pivot about their ankles), while the first player to drop the 'walrus' loses and becomes the next 'carcass'.]

♦

The game of *Chinese whispers*, in which a message is relayed secretly from player to player, was previously called 'Russian scandal'.

♦

Scandal derives from the Latin for 'stumbling block'. In Ancient Greece, it was a trap for a wild animal.

♦

In nineteenth-century American slang, a *wolf-trap* was a low-cost or corrupt casino.

♦

Casino means 'little house' in Italian.

[*Casino* was first used in the mid-1700s to refer to a clubhouse where various musical acts and dances would be performed. It wasn't until the mid-1800s that it came to be used almost exclusively for a gambling house, with the shift in meaning probably partly motivated by a card game called *cassino* that was popular at the turn of the eighteenth century.

It might come as little surprise to find that the earliest record of a gambler's *casino* in English also provides us the earliest reference to someone losing a vast amount of money in one: while holidaying in France on 15 August 1851, Effie Ruskin, the wife of the Victorian artist and critic John Ruskin, wrote home to England to report that Sir Robert Peel Jr, the eldest son of the former British Prime Minister Sir Robert Peel, had 'lost in gambling at Chamouni [Chamonix] to the Master of the Casino 25,000 francs'.]

♦

Roulette means 'little wheel' in French.

♦

A *wheeler* is someone who attends an auction to bid on items merely to increase their sale price.

[Other names for a deceitful vendor's associate include *pot-plant*, *setter*, *showman*, *ampster* and *quhysselar*, a Scots transmogrification *wisseler*, namely someone who changes money from one currency to another. *Wheeler-dealer* is a more recent invention dating from the early 1960s.]

♦

A *wheel-horse* is the person who bears the greatest burden of a business or enterprise.

♦

A *horse's-neck* is a spirit (usually whisky or brandy) mixed with ginger ale and lemon.

♦

To drown the miller means 'to mix too much water into a drink'.

♦

The Icelandic word for a hangover, *timburmenn*, means 'carpenters'.

[*Timburmenn* literally means 'timber-men', but has come to refer to a hangover in Icelandic in the sense of a continuous hammering pain. Hangovers are apparently just as bad in Sweden, where the headache associated with drinking too much is called a *kopparslagare*, or a 'coppersmith'. Elsewhere, in Germany a hangover is either a *Kater*, meaning 'tomcat', or a *Katzenjammer*, literally a 'caterwauling'. The French talk of having a *gueule de bois*, or 'wooden mouth', after too much *eau de vie*, and in some parts of the Spanish-speaking world you might well wake up feeling like a *guayabo*, or a 'guava tree'.]

♦

There are no surnames in Icelandic.

[The second part of most native Icelanders' names are patronymics rather than surnames, and so are based around their fathers' names (or occasionally their mothers') with the addition of either *–son* or *–dóttir* for a 'son' or 'daughter'. Icelandic children ultimately tend to have different second names to their parents, and a person's first name is usually seen as their most important – even the Icelandic phone book is listed by first rather than second name, with people's occupations listed alongside their addresses to help differentiate between duplicates.]

♦

The surname *Kennedy* means 'ugly-head'.

[He topped a 2009 poll to be named the best-looking President in US history, but JFK's surname is actually the Old Irish epithet *ceannéidigh*, derived from *ceann*, meaning 'head', and *éidigh*, meaning 'ugly'.]

♦

The Japanese word *bushusuru* means 'to vomit in public' – as President George Bush Sr did on a state visit to Japan in 1992.

> [While attending a banquet in Tokyo with the Japanese Prime Minister, Miyazawa Kiichi, on 8 January 1992, President George H. W. Bush suddenly vomited before promptly passing out. The President had apparently taken ill earlier that day and had been advised by his doctor to remain in bed, but he decided to attend the banquet undaunted and as a result the whole unfortunate event – later blamed on a 24-hour stomach bug – was caught on camera and broadcast around the world. Newspapers from the time record how within days Japanese teenagers had coined *bushusuru* – literally 'to do a Bush'.]

♦

A *maw-wallop* is an unpleasant mixture of random foods or drinks consumed only to make someone sick.

♦

Shakespeare used the word *puking* in *As You Like It*.

> [Not only that, but Shakespeare used *puking* in one of his most celebrated speeches, the 'All the world's a stage' monologue in *As You Like It* (II.vii). The speech famously compares a lifetime of events to the dramas acted out by players on a stage, beginning with 'the infant, / Mewling and puking in the nurse's arms', and ending with 'second childishness', and 'mere oblivion, / Sans teeth, sans eyes, sans taste, sans everything'.]

♦

Nauseous means 'causing nausea'. *Nauseated* means 'feeling sick'. So saying 'I'm nauseous' means 'I'm making other people sick'.

A Roman *vomitorium* was an entrance to an amphitheatre, not a room in which diners intentionally made themselves sick.

> [The idea that the Romans withdrew to a *vomitorium* after a feast for a bushusuru before recommencing eating is a twentieth-century myth, likely based on nothing more than the word *vomitorium* itself. In fact, the verb *vomere* was used to mean both 'vomit' and merely 'expel' or 'stream out' in Latin, and so a true vomitorium was merely the part of a public building through which an audience would 'stream' in or out.]

A *dimachaerus* was a gladiator with two swords. A *laquearius* was a gladiator with a lasso and a sword. A *retiarius* was a gladiator with a net and a trident.

> [*Gladiator* simply means 'sword-fighter', and in Ancient Rome there were numerous different subtypes of gladiatorial fighter each named after their weapon of choice or their area of expertise. A *scissor*, for instance, was a gladiator armed with a dual-bladed, Y-shaped knife. A *sagittarius* was armed with a bow and arrow, sometimes on horseback. A *bestiarius* was a specialised 'beast-fighter', who would battle bears and lions rather than human opponents. And a *cestus* was a fist-fighter, armed with nothing more than a studded or spiked leather glove.]

Reticulated means 'net-like' – *reticulated pythons* are named after the net-like pattern on their scales.

Adders were originally called 'nadders'. *Umpires* were originally called 'numpires'. *Aprons* were originally called 'naprons'.

[The initial Ns of 'nadder', 'napron' and 'numpire' were all lost in the early Middle Ages, when they were misguidedly altered to 'an adder', 'an apron' and 'an umpire'. This process is called rebracketing or metanalysis, and also accounts for the initial Ns gained by words like *nickname* and *newt* when their earlier forms, 'an eke-name' and 'an eute', were similarly misread. A 'numpire', incidentally, was originally a *nonper* (i.e. 'not-equal'), implying a third person brought in to judge between two others.]

◆

Apron and *napkin* both mean 'little tablecloth'.

◆

A butcher's table is called a *shamble*. A *shambles* was originally a meat market or street of butchers' shops.

◆

A *cagbutcher* is a butcher who sells poor quality meat from wild or diseased animals.

◆

One theory claims that *Eskimo* means 'eater of raw meat'.

[No one is entirely sure what the word *Eskimo* means, but the most widely held theory is that it comes from an Algonquin word, *askipiw*, meaning something like 'eater of raw meat', or 'he eats it raw'. French settlers arriving in Canada in the sixteenth century would have picked this word up from the tribes they encountered on the coast, and ultimately used their Frenchified version of it, *esquimaux*, to describe the tribes that inhabited the colder regions further north. (*Frenchified* is a perfectly acceptable word dating back to the seventeenth century.)]

◆

Acharnment is ruthless, unstoppable enthusiasm. It derives from a French word meaning 'to give hounds a taste of meat before a hunt'.

◆

In Malay, dogs say *gong-gong*. In Korean, they say *meong-meong*. In Mandarin, they say *wang-wang*.

◆

A *growlery* is anywhere you like to retreat to when you're ill or in a bad mood.

[It'll come as little surprise to discover that such a superb word as *growlery* was coined by Charles Dickens, and first appeared in his novel *Bleak House* in 1853:

'Sit down, my dear', said Mr Jarndyce. 'This, you must know, is the Growlery. When I am out of humour, I come and growl here.'
'You must be here very seldom, sir,' said I.
'Oh, you don't know me!' he returned.]

◆

Vernalagnia is a good mood brought on by the return of fine weather in the spring.

[*Vernalagnia* is the proper name for what is otherwise known as 'spring fever', a brighter and often romantic change of mood brought on by the change of season – or, as one nineteenth-century *Dictionary of Americanisms* put it, 'the listless feeling caused by the first sudden increase of temperature in spring'. The root of the word is the Greek for 'lust', *lagneia*, from which are derived a whole host of less wholesome (often fairly niche) attractions and fetishes: *iconolagnia* is an attraction to semi-clad statues and figurines; an *ecdemolagnic* is someone who prefers being away from home to being in their own bedroom; and a *tripsolagnic* is someone who enjoys having their hair shampooed just that little bit too much.]

◆

The opposite of *hibernation* is *estivation* – sleeping for an entire summer.

◆

The place a hibernating animal sleeps is its *hibernacle*.

◆

An *expergefactor* is anything that wakes you up in the morning.

◆

Clinomania is an excessive desire to stay in bed. *Dysania* is an inability to get out of bed. *Matutolypea* is an early morning bad mood.

◆

Antelucan means 'occurring before dawn'. *Crepuscular* means 'occurring at twilight'. *Mesonoxian* means 'occurring at midnight'.

♦

In Tudor England, midnight was also known as *noontide*.

♦

'To look for noon at 2 p.m.' – *chercher midi à quatorze heures* – means 'to make something more complicated' in French.

♦

Noon was originally 3 p.m.

> [*Noon* is a corruption of the Latin word for 'ninth', *novem*, and originally referred to the ninth hour of the Roman day – reckoned by modern clocks to have been around 3 p.m. *Noon* was first used in this sense in the Old English period, before it finally came to refer to midday in the early Middle Ages. Precisely what motivated the change from 3 to 12 o'clock remains a mystery.]

♦

In Canadian slang, someone who wastes time is called an *afternoon farmer*.

♦

Earthling meant 'ploughman' in Old English.

♦

An *oxgang* is an area of roughly 15–20 acres – the amount of farmland an ox can plough in one day.

♦

Bucephalus, the name of Alexander the Great's horse, means 'ox-headed'.

♦

The Albanian currency, the *lek*, is named after Alexander the Great.

♦

The former Greek currency, the *drachma*, literally means 'handful'.

♦

The 'bowl' formed by cupping your hands is called a *gowpen*. The amount it holds is called a *yepsen*.

♦

The earliest known reference to a *bowling alley* dates from 1555.

> [Bowling was a hugely popular pastime in Tudor England, and even Henry VIII had an enormous 200-ft bowling alley installed at Hampton Court shortly after the birth of Edward VI. By the time Mary I came to the throne in 1553, however, the rowdy behaviour of bowlers, gamers and gamblers was beginning to prove a problem on the streets of London, and in 1555 an Act of Parliament (which provides the earliest known record of a *bowling alley*) was introduced that sought to repeal:
>
> > every License, Placard, or Grant made to any Person or Persons for the having, Maintenance, or keeping of any Bowling-allies, Dicing-houses, or other unlawful Games, prohibited by the laws and statutes of this Realm.]

♦

During the First World War, Germans were nicknamed *Alleymen*.

> [*Alleyman* is an anglicised version of the French name for Germany, *Allemagne*, which is in turn derived from the name of an ancient European tribe called the Alemanni. Its earliest use in print has been dated to 1915, but it's likely the nickname was in use before then in the lyrics of wartime and trenches songs like this one:
>
>> I want to go home, I want to go home.
>> I don't want to be in the trenches no more,
>> Where whizz-bangs and shrapnel, they whistle and roar.
>> Take me over the sea, where the Alleyman can't get at me.]

♦

In Navajo, Germany is called *Béésh Bich'ahii Bikéyah* – or 'metal cap-wearer land'.

♦

The German word *kummerspeck* means 'excess weight gained through comfort eating'. It literally means 'grief-bacon'.

♦

A *rorschgramm* is a butchers' unit of weight equal to the amount of fat in one side of a fully-grown pig.

♦

The French word for a pig's snout is *groin*.

♦

Pigs don't *oink* in Czech, they say *chro*. In Albanian they say *hunk*. In Norwegian they say *nøff*.

◆

Norwegian steam is an old American slang name for manpower or brute strength.

◆

The engineer James Watt defined one *horsepower* as the amount of power needed to lift a weight of 33,000 lb by a height of 1 ft in one minute.

> [In the late eighteenth century, engineers looking to market improvements in steam technology needed an easy means of demonstrating how their inventions compared to what was, at the time, the most widely used tool for heavy or demanding work: the horse. Watt's *horsepower* unit was an attempt to do just that, and was based on his observation of a horse, that was able to lift 180 lbs, turning a 75 ft-circumference millwheel 144 times in one hour. This meant the wheel travelled 181 ft each minute, and given a pulling force of 180 lbs, enabled Watt to define the horse's 'power' as roughly 33,000 foot-pounds-per-minute. One *horsepower*, ultimately, was the power required to match that of one horse and so raise a 33,000 lb load by 1 ft (or a 330 lb load by 100 ft, or a 33 lb load by 1,000 ft, and so on) in one minute. Nowadays, Watt's calculations are considered somewhat optimistic (a horse could hardly be expected to pull with a 180 lb force continuously, and some explanations have suggested his estimations were as much as fifty per cent out), but his innovative *horsepower* unit nevertheless remains in use to this day.]

◆

In the Middle Ages, *seconds* were known as 'second minutes'.

◆

The two dots written above the second vowel in words like 'Zoë' and 'naïve' is called a *diaeresis*.

[This double-dot diacritic is often wrongly referred to as an *umlaut*, which is an identical symbol used in a completely different way. Specifically, a *diaeresis* is used to show that the vowel in question needs to be pronounced independently from the one before it – thereby ensuring *Zoë* rhymes with 'doughy', not 'toe'. Although its use is more complex, the *umlaut* is essentially used to show that the corresponding vowel has a different pronunciation than it would normally – so the *ü* of *Zürich* sounds like the *u* in 'mute', not the *u* in 'but'.]

◆

A æ u å æ ø i æ å means 'I am on the island in the stream' in Jysk, the dialect of Danish spoken in Jutland.

◆

The longest English word comprised only of vowels is *euouae*, the name of a type of cadence in mediaeval plainsong.

[*Euouae* is hardly the most familiar or useful of words today (unless you're sitting with a particularly unlucky collection of Scrabble tiles), nevertheless it refers to the standard pattern or cadence of notes that ended the *Gloria Patri*, a prayer that was popular in mediaeval plainsong. It's derived from the alternating vowels of the prayer's last two words, *seculorum amen* – and for precisely that reason some lexicographers class *euouae* as an abbreviation rather than a word in its own right. If so, then the longest vowel-only word becomes *aieee*, 'a wailing exclamation of resignation' according to the *Oxford English Dictionary*, followed by *euoi*, 'a cry of impassioned rapture'.]

♦

Aegilops, a type of eye ulcer, is the longest English word with its letters in alphabetical order.

[Words with their letters in alphabetical order aren't actually as rare as this fairly peculiar example might suggest, and in fact a full list of them would include such familiar terms as *accept*, *billowy*, *chilly*, *chimps*, *effort*, *floors* and *knotty*. The longest word with its letters in reverse alphabetical order is *spoonfeed*, closely followed by *trollied*, *sponged*, *spooked*, *sniffed* and *wronged*.]

♦

An *abecedarian* or an *ABCdarian* is someone who is learning the alphabet.

♦

The Cambodian alphabet has seventy-four letters.

♦

Four has four letters. It's the only self-describing number in the English language.

[In some dialects of Middle English and Scots, the word for 'one' was reduced simply to o, or even 'n in some contexts, but these examples are so obsolete and unusual that they can be excluded here. Self-describing numbers in other languages, however, include *u* (Catalan); *to* (Danish, Norwegian); *tre* (Italian); *vier* (German); *cinco* (Spanish, Portuguese); *hastąą* (Navajo); *septyni* (Lithuanian); *kekjamys* (Komi, a language of northern Russia); *bederatzi* (Basque); and *wumutirnra* (Tiwi, an Aboriginal language spoken only on the Tiwi Islands off Australia's north coast).

As the numbers climb ever higher, self-describing numbers become understandably scarcer, but highest of all is probably the twenty-two-letter Zulu word for 'twenty-two', *amashumi amabili nambili*.]

♦

A *carfax* is another name for a crossroads, or a place where four or more roads meet.

♦

Trivia derives from a Latin word for a place where three roads meet.

[*Via* means 'way' in Latin, both in the sense of 'by way of' and 'road' or 'pathway', and so a *trivium* is literally a place where three roads or paths come together, and a *quadrivium* is a crossroads. These two terms came to be used metaphorically across mediaeval Europe for the two main branches of learning, known collectively as the Seven Liberal Arts: the *quadrivium* comprised the four so-called 'mathematical sciences' of arithmetic, geometry, astronomy and music, and the *trivium* comprised grammar, rhetoric and logic. This latter group was seen as the lower or less important of the two, and hence *trivia* (the plural of *trivium*) eventually came to mean any inconsequential details or quaint titbits of information. Precisely like this one.]

♦

An *ambivium* is a road or pathway that runs around something, rather than up to it.

♦

To *circumambulate* means 'to walk all the way around something, especially in order to fully appreciate or assess it'.

[The 'circum' of *circumambulation* is a Latin word meaning 'around' or 'on all sides', from which words like *circumference* and *circumnavigate* are likewise derived. To *circumambulate* ultimately means 'to walk around' something, but in practice the word is often used in religious and ceremonial contexts to refer to worshipers and devotees respectfully circling some kind of idol or symbol as part of a traditional ritual. In more figurative use, however, *circumambulate* can also be used to mean to talk long-windedly, or to procrastinate and beat about the bush.]

◆

To walk *Newgate fashion* means 'to walk hand in hand', as inmates shackled together at London's Newgate prison would once have done.

[A prison of some shape or form stood on the site of the 'new gate' in London's Roman wall from 1188 until 1904. It was by all accounts an appalling place:

> 'tis impossible to describe the terror of my mind, when I was first brought in ... the hellish noise, the roaring, swearing, and clamour, the stench and nastiness, and all the dreadful crowd of afflicting things that I saw there, joined together to make the place seem an emblem of hell itself, and a kind of entrance to it.
>
> — *Moll Flanders* (1722), Daniel Defoe

Originally built on the orders of Henry II, the first Newgate prison was destroyed by the Great Fire in 1666. Its replacement lasted another century, until it too was destroyed by riots in 1780. Undeterred, Newgate was reconstructed and reopened in 1782, just in time for London's public gallows to be moved there from Tyburn in the city's West End. This final incarnation of the prison, and its longstanding association with its scaffolds, is at the heart of most of the 'Newgate' phrases used in English: a *Newgate fringe* is a beard or curl of long hair that encircles the neck like a noose, while the *Newgate hornpipe* is the 'dancing legs' of a man being hanged. *Newgate fashion* is a much earlier expression however, first used by Shakespeare in *Henry IV: Part 1*.]

♦

A *panopticon* is a circular prison arranged so that all of the inmates can be permanently observed from a central point.

[*Panopticon* means 'all-seeing' in Greek, and in the early 1700s was the name given to all sorts of optical devices, including several early picture-viewers and projectors. All that changed in 1787, when the English philosopher and social reformer Jeremy Bentham proposed his idea for an enormous circular prison that allowed for constant surveillance of its inmates, who would be held in isolation in scores of individual cells. He wrote in 1791:

In a Panopticon prison there ought not anywhere be a single foot square, on which man or boy shall be able to plant himself – no not for a moment – under any assurance of not being observed.

After a decade of campaigning, Bentham's design was finally accepted in 1794 and plans were passed by Parliament to build a panopticon, acting as a new National Penitentiary, at Millbank in London. The plans, however, were abandoned in 1812 and the final building was not constructed to Bentham's extraordinary specifications.]

♦

The first *treadmill* was a vast man-powered mill designed to crush rocks and grind corn. It was used as a hard labour punishment in Victorian prisons.

♦

Dumbbells were originally weighted ropes not bars, so-called because they resembled the ropes used to ring church bells.

♦

Bellini cocktails are named after the Italian artist Giovanni Bellini, who used a similar peach colour in one of his paintings.

> [A classic *Bellini* is a mix of sparkling wine and peach purée, which gives the drink its traditional orange colour. It was this that reminded the drink's inventor, Giuseppe Cipriani, of a colour frequently used in the artist Bellini's works – such as that of the robes worn by Moses in the *Transfiguration of Christ* (circa 1480) – and the name has remained in use ever since.]

♦

Because its flowers change colour from one day to the next, the shrub *Brunfelsia bonodora* is nicknamed *yesterday-today-tomorrow*.

♦

To *perendinate* is to put something off until the day after tomorrow.

♦

The day after tomorrow is the *other morrow*.

♦

In Urdu, the same word, *kal*, is used to mean both 'tomorrow' and 'yesterday'.

◆

Using the same word or phrase at the beginning and end of a sentence – like 'the king is dead, long live the king' – is called *epanalepsis*.

[*Epanalepsis* literally means 'taking up again' or 'repetition' in Greek, and is the same figure of speech that helps to make 'Nice to see you, to see you nice' such a memorable turn of phrase. It's different from *anadiplosis*, in which a word or phrase is repeated at the end of one line and the beginning of the next, and *anaphora*, in which the same word or phrase is used at the beginning of a series clauses:

It was the best of times, it was the worst of times, it was the age of wisdom, it was the age of foolishness, it was the epoch of belief, it was the epoch of incredulity, it was the season of Light, it was the season of Darkness, it was the spring of hope, it was the winter of despair...

— *A Tale of Two Cities* (1859), Charles Dickens]

◆

Checkmate derives from *shah-mat*, the Arabic for 'the king is dead'.

[Remarkably, almost every use of the word *check* in English is somehow derived from chess. (In fact, the only one listed in the *Oxford English Dictionary* that isn't is an eighteenth-century nickname for the wheatear, a bird of the flycatcher family.) *Check* itself was adopted from the French word for 'chess', *eschec*, and first appeared in the fourteenth century as a player's call to his opponent that his king has been 'checked' and that he is in danger of losing the game. From this original meaning came *check* to mean 'a stoppage', 'a reprimand', 'an obstruction', 'a restraint', 'a control', 'an assessment', and 'a proof of accuracy or legitimacy' (from which *cheque*, in the financial sense, eventually emerged). As a verb – variously meaning 'to stop', 'to block', 'to curb', 'to test' or 'to ensure' – every use of *check* derives from its equivalent noun. And even *exchequer* can be traced back to a chessboard-patterned cloth on which mediaeval revenue-takers would count out and arrange their finances.]

♦

A *gambit* is not just a gamble – it's a type of chess opening in which a player must sacrifice a pawn in order to gain an advantage.

♦

A *woodpusher* is a poor chess player.

♦

Bishop is a drink of 'wine and water, into which is put a roasted orange'.

[The description above is taken from Francis Grose's *Dictionary of the Vulgar Tongue* (1785), which stopped short of pointing out that *bishop* was apparently a favourite tipple of Samuel Johnson:

One night [in 1752], when Beauclerk and Langton had supped at a tavern in London, and sat till about three in the morning, it came into their heads to go and knock up Johnson, and see if they could prevail on him to join them in a ramble. They rapped violently at the doors of his chambers … till at last he appeared in his shirt, with his little black wig on the top of his head instead of a nightcap, and a poker in his hand, imagining, probably, that some ruffians were coming to attack him. When he discovered who they were, and was told their errand, he smiled, and with great good humour agreed to their proposal: 'What, is it you, you dogs! I'll have a frisk with you.' … They then repaired to one of the neighbouring taverns, and made a bowl of that liquor called Bishop, which Johnson had always liked ... They did not stay long, but walked down to the Thames, took a boat, and rowed to Billingsgate. Beauclerk and Johnson were so well pleased with their amusement, that they resolved to persevere in dissipation for the rest of the day; but Langton deserted them, being engaged to breakfast with some young ladies. Johnson scolded him for 'leaving his social friends, to go and sit with a set of un-idea'd girls'.

The Life of Samuel Johnson (1791), James Boswell]

♦

An *ale-knight* is a drinking companion, or a habitual drunkard.

♦

A *shot-log* is an unwanted friend or drinking companion, whose company is only tolerated so that they can pay for a round for the rest of the group.

♦

In Tudor England, a *morning-draught* was an alcoholic drink taken with or instead of breakfast.

♦

The earliest reference to *the hair of the dog* as a cure for a hangover dates from 1546.

[The idea that 'a hair of a dog' has some kind of curative property comes from the ancient theory that bites from wild or rabid animals could be treated by binding the wound with the creature's fur. By the time the Tudor period came around, however, this 'treatment' had become little more than a humorous name for drinking to cure a hangover (thereby using a cause as a cure), leading the English writer John Heywood to include the following in his collection of *Proverbs in the English Tongue* (1546):

> I praie the leat me and my felowe haue A heare of the dog that bote vs last nygh.
> [*I prithee, let me and my fellow have a hair of the dog that bit us last night.*]

That's not to say that this was a purely English habit of course, as the lexicographer Randle Cotgrave included this entry under 'beast' in his *Dictionarie of the French and English Tongues* (1611):

> *Prendre du poil de la beste.* To take a remedie for a mischiefe from that which was the cause thereof; as to go thin clothed when a cold is taken; or in drunkenness to fall a-quaffing, thereby to recover health, or sobrietie, neere unto which sense our Ale-knights often use this phrase, and say, Give us a haire of the dog that bit us.

But does it work? Well, various pseudoscientific theories claim that alcohol is better at breaking down the toxins that are present in higher levels in the body when you're hungover than the body's enzymes are themselves – but why get technical when you've Samuel Pepys on your side?

> [3 April 1661] ...my head akeing all day from last night's debauch. ... at noon dined with Sir W. Batten and Pen, who would needs have me drink two drafts [*sic*] of sack to-day to cure me of last night's disease, which I thought strange, but I think find it true.]

◆

Anyone who is *crambazzled* has aged prematurely through excessive drinking.

◆

Anyone who is *semperjuvenescent* is always appearing to be getting younger.

♦

An *ephebe* is someone aged between 18 and 20: in Ancient Greece, the *epheboi* were young men who had their hair shaved off ready for military service at the age of 18.

♦

Compulsively pulling out your hair is called *trichotillomania*. Obsessively playing with your hair is called *trichomania*. Compulsively picking your nose is called *rhinotillexomania*.

♦

To *Coventry* someone means to slit their nose.

[This is different from *being sent to Coventry*, meaning 'to ostracise', the origins of which are shrouded in mystery. Instead this even grimmer use of *Coventry* derives from Sir John Coventry, an English politician who, on 21 December 1670, had the gall to suggest that Parliament should begin levying a tax on playhouses. In opposition the point was raised that London's theatres had been 'of great pleasure to the king', Charles II, to which Coventry was quick to question whether 'the King's pleasure lay among the men or the women that acted' – a less-than-subtle reference to Charles' on-going romance with the 20-year-old actress Nell Gwyn. Although Sir John's comment was apparently meant as nothing more than a satirical joke, the Duke of Monmouth, one of the King's closest friends and allies, happened to overhear it and failed to see the funny side. On the Duke's orders, Sir John was ambushed as he walked home later that night by a group of the king's guards, who reportedly slit his nose down to the bone beneath. The attack unsurprisingly caused outrage in the capital, and quickly led to an Act of Parliament that imposed the death penalty on anyone who sought to 'unlawfully cut out or disable the tongue, put out an eye, slit the nose, cut off a nose or lip, or cut off or disable any limb or member of any Subject of His Majesty'. The Coventry Act, as it became known, remained in force until 1828.]

●

The groove in the upper lip just below the nose is called the *philtrum*. It's derived from the Greek word for a love-charm.

●

Aphrodisiacs take their name from Aphrodite, the Greek goddess of love.

●

Venom is related to Venus, the Roman goddess of love. It was probably originally a name for a love potion.

●

Toxin derives from the Greek word for an archer's bow, *toxon*. It was probably originally a name for poison-tipped arrows.

●

In the Middle Ages, a *pluck-buffet* was an archery competition in which the winner was allowed to hit the loser over the head.

[The earliest record of a *pluck-buffet* comes from a lengthy 1,800-line poem called *A Gest of Robyn Hode* first published in 1510 – although the folktales on which it was probably based date back as far as the early 1300s. The poem tells of a meeting between Robin Hood and the King of England (in this case Edward II) who has disguised himself as a monk in order to trap Robin:

> Our kynge and Robyn rode togyder,
> For soth as I you say,
> And they shote plucke-buffet
> As they went by the way[.]

While playing a round of 'plucke-buffet', Robin misses the target and as a forfeit must 'bere a buffet on his hede'. The king delivers such a suspiciously and mercilessly strong blow to Robin's head, however, that Robin immediately sees through his disguise and, with no chance of escape, he and his men fall to their knees and beg for mercy. In return the king offers them positions at his court in lieu of punishment and they spend the next fifteen months in his service in Nottingham until Robin eventually absconds and returns to life as an outlaw in Sherwood Forest.]

◆

A *fistmele* is a unit of length equal to the size of a clenched fist with the thumb extended. It was once considered the perfect distance between an archer's bow and its bowstring.

◆

The L-shape formed between the thumb and forefinger is called the *purlicue*.

◆

The ring finger was once called the *nameless finger*, the *leech-finger*, and the *medicinal finger*.

♦

A *lapsus digitorum* – literally a 'slip of the finger' – is a spelling mistake made by someone using sign language.

♦

The most commonly misspelled word in the English language is *separate*.

[A survey in 2010 found that *separate* – typically misspelled with an E in place of the first A – was the most troublesome word in the English language, seeing off competition from the likes of *definitely* in second place, and *manoeuvre* in third. Elsewhere, combinations of double and single letters seemingly proved difficult (*embarrass, occurrence, unnecessary* and *broccoli* all made the top 20), as well as easily confusable Cs and Ss (*consensus, supersede, conscience*) and a handful of foreign borrowings (*connoisseur, entrepreneur*). Curiously, the fifteenth most commonly misspelled word in English is *a lot*.]

♦

Before decimal points, a line or slash called a *separatrix* was used instead.

[The decimal point is a relatively modern addition to European arithmetic that was adopted from ancient Arabic and Indian texts in the sixteenth and seventeenth centuries and championed by the likes of John Napier, the inventor of logarithms. Before then, decimal figures were separated from whole numbers by a vertical line or slash, like 12|34 or 12/34, or else were identified by an L-shaped (⌐) or horizontal bar (‾) which would be written above the last whole number in a sequence – so 12.34 would be written 12‾34. The name *separatrix* initially only applied to the symbols (⁀) or (⁔) before coming to refer to any symbol, including the decimal point itself, which divides whole numbers from fractions.]

♦

The line separating the numbers in a fraction is called a *vinculum*.

[*Vinculum* means 'bond' or 'tie' in Latin, and in mathematics is used to refer not only to the line dividing a fraction, but to any line that shows a number or series of numbers can be considered as a group. Recurring decimals such as 0.33333 … for instance, can be shortened to 0.3̄.]

♦

An *isoceraunic* line is one drawn on a weather map linking places with an equal frequency of thunderstorms per year.

♦

Jiffy is thought to have originally been a slang name for a flash of lightning.

[The earliest written record of the word *jiffy* dates it to 1785, when it appeared in *The Surprising Adventures of Baron Munchausen* by Rudolph Erich Raspe:

away we went, helter-skelter, and in six jiffies I found myself and all my retinue, safe and in good spirits, at the rock of Gibraltar.

As a slang word for lightning, *jiffy* or *jeffy* has been dated to the early 1800s in written English, but it was likely in use in spoken English considerably earlier, suggesting the two meanings are probably related. The US scientist Gilbert N. Lewis took this idea even further in 1916, when he suggested that a *jiffy* should be precisely defined as 33.3564 picoseconds (roughly three-trillionths of a second) – namely the time it takes light to travel one centimetre.]

●

A *moment* is precisely a fortieth of an hour.

[*Moment* is descended from the Latin word for 'movement', *momentum*, and is said to have originally referred to the smallest quantity of something – literally a grain or crumb – that was capable of moving the pointer of a scale. This in turn came to be applied to the movements of the hands of a clock, and a *moment* soon became simply another name for a short amount of time. The precise duration of a *moment* was inconsistent until the thirteenth century, when the Franciscan scholar Bartholomeus Anglicus explained in his great encyclopaedia, *De Proprietatibus Rerum* ('On the Properties of Things'), that:

> An hour [comprises] four points, and a point ten moments, and a moment twelve ounces, and an ounce forty-seven atoms.

By Bartholomeus's reckoning, a quarter of an hour is a *point*; a tenth of a point is a *moment*, or ninety seconds; an *ounce* is a twelfth of a moment, or seven and a half seconds; and an *atom* (derived from the Greek for 'uncuttable') is a 376th of a minute, or about 160 milliseconds – the shortest, literally 'undividable', amount of time.]

●

A *smidgen* is precisely ⅟₃₂ of a teaspoon.

[Both *smidge* and *smidgen* are thought to be derived from any one of a number of nineteenth-century dialect words including *smoot* or *smitch* (old Scots words for insignificant amounts), and *smiddum* or *smitham* (old miners' terms for tiny particles or remnants of lead ore). In recent years however, *smidgen* has been adopted by American manufacturers of kitchen equipment to refer to the smallest measuring spoon in a standard set, which holds precisely a thirty-second of a teaspoon.

A *pinch* by comparison is a sixteenth of a teaspoon, while a *dash* is an eighth.]

♦

A *koku* is a Japanese measurement equal to approximately 278 litres – or the quantity of rice required to feed a person for one year.

♦

The *Oxford English Dictionary* defines a *food coma* as 'a state of sleep or extreme lethargy induced by the consumption of a large amount of food'.

♦

An *idioticon* is a dictionary of a dialect or minority language.

♦

As an example of how to use the word *dull*, Samuel Johnson's *Dictionary* states, 'to make dictionaries is dull work'.

♦

Fiffle-fafflement is dull, trifling, time-wasting work.

♦

Bumph, meaning 'tiresome or pointless work', is a military nickname for toilet paper. It's shortened from 'bum-fodder'.

In eighteenth-century England, bailiffs were nicknamed *bumtraps*.

[It was Shakespeare who first contemptuously referred to *bumbailiffs* in *Twelfth Night* (III.iv), likely in reference to the fact that bailiffs are always on their debtors' 'tails'. Samuel Johnson quoted Shakespeare in his dictionary and explained that as a prefix, *bum-* is used to refer to 'any thing mean or low', defining a *bumbailiff* as 'a bailiff of the meanest kind; one that is employed in arrests'. But it was Henry Fielding who dealt the strongest blow in his scathing description of a cruel and unsympathetic bailiff in his novel *Tom Jones* (1749): 'The noble bumtrap, blind and deaf to every circumstance of distress, greatly rises above all the motives to humanity, and into the hands of the gaoler resolves to deliver his miserable prey.']

To *bumfuzzle* someone is to confuse them.

A *fuzzword* is a deliberately ambiguous word used to mislead someone.

The *Papua* of 'Papua New Guinea' is supposedly a Malay word, *papuah*, meaning 'fuzzy-haired'.

A *Struwwelpeter* is someone with wildly uncontrollable hair, named after an unkempt character from German folklore.

Cobalt was once considered so poisonous to miners that it was named after the *kobold*, an invisible goblin from German folklore.

[The two main ores of cobalt – cobaltite and smaltite – both contain an equal amount of arsenic, making mining for them a particularly hazardous business. Long before the harmful nature of certain metals was known to science, the miners who fell ill or even died from collecting cobalt would have had little explanation for the illnesses or irritations it caused and as a result turned to the supernatural, blaming subterranean goblins or *kobolds*, whom they believed lived inside the rock. As Sir Walter Scott explained in his *Letters on Demonology and Witchcraft* (1830):

The Kobolds were a species of gnomes, who haunted the dark and solitary places, and were often seen in the mines, where they seemed to imitate the labours of the miners, and sometimes took pleasure in frustrating their objects and rendering their toil unfruitful. Sometimes they were malignant, especially if neglected or insulted; but sometimes also they were indulgent to individuals whom they took under their protection. When a miner, therefore, hit upon a rich vein of ore, the inference commonly was, not that he possessed more skill, industry, or even luck, than his fellow-workmen but that the spirits of the mine had directed him to the treasure.]

Copernicus, Albert Einstein, Pierre and Marie Curie, Ernest Rutherford and Alfred Nobel all have chemical elements named after them.

[Besides *copernicium* (atomic number 112), *einsteinium* (99), *curium* (96), *rutherfordium* (104) and *nobelium* (102), the periodic table also commemorates Enrico Fermi (*fermium*, 100), Niels Bohr (*bohrium*, 107) and Wilhelm Roentgen (*roentgenium*, 111), alongside several notable scientific figures. Appropriately enough, chemical element number 101, *mendelevium*, is named in honour of the Russian chemist Dmitri Mendeleev, who published one of the earliest recorded versions of the periodic table in 1869.]

♦

The element *praseodymium* derives from a Greek word meaning 'leek-green'.

♦

References to colours are so rare in Ancient Greek literature that some nineteenth-century scholars presumed that they must only have been able to see in black and white.

[This peculiar theory is usually credited to William Gladstone, who as well as being a former British Prime Minister was also a renowned classicist. Gladstone outlined his ideas on the Ancient Greeks' use (or rather disuse) of colour in his *Studies on Homer and the Homeric Age*, published while he was MP for Oxford University in 1858:

> The materials, therefore, for a system of colour did not offer them-selves to Homer's vision as they do to ours … I conclude, then, that the organ of colour and its impressions were but partially developed among the Greeks of the heroic age.

According to Homer, the sea in *The Odyssey* wasn't blue but 'wine-dark'. Sheep and oxen too were 'wine-coloured', while the sky was bronze, honey and nightingales were leaf-green, and Hector's hair in *The Iliad* was dark blue. Given as apparently skewed a palette as this, it's easy to see where Gladstone's theory comes from, but unsurpris-ingly modern classicists tend not to agree. Instead, they argue that

Homer and his contemporaries' choices of words were never meant to be translated as colours themselves, but rather as shades or gradients of colours implied by the text – you *know* the sea is blue, so by calling it 'wine-dark' Homer doesn't mean that it looks like red wine, it just implies a much richer and deeper blue than you might otherwise imagine. Alternatively, this could be an issue of resources: perhaps the Ancient Greek vocabulary simply wasn't robust enough to supply its writers with enough words for all of the colours and shades that we have the luxury of being able to describe today. After all, exactly how can you describe the colour of honey if none of the words you have at your disposal is appropriate? Or perhaps ancient writers didn't consider colour as important an attribute as modern writers do? Whatever the reason may be, the whole issue remains one big grey area.]

♦

A black and white horse is called a *piebald*. A brown and white horse is called a *skewbald*.

[The Old English word for 'bald' was *callow* (which now means 'inexperienced' or 'youthful', thanks to an association with hairless newborns and featherless birds), while *bald* didn't come to mean 'hairless' until the fourteenth century. Before then, it meant 'a patch of white hair', particularly one on the head or face of a horse, from which words like *piebald* and *skewbald* have since derived.]

♦

The surname *Mulligan* means 'little bald man'.

♦

In golf, a *mulligan* is a replayed shot that is allowed without a penalty.

[*Mulligan* is an Irish surname believed to derive from *maol*, meaning 'bald', and so was probably originally an epithet bestowed on some notable shaven-headed monk or abbot. How it came to be used in golf is the subject of several myths and tall tales, but the most likely explanation is that it derives from a Canadian golfer named David B. Mulligan, who is said to have introduced the term in the 1930s.]

●

Golf isn't an acronym of 'gentlemen only, ladies forbidden'.

[Nor for that matter does *golf* stand for 'gentlemen only, ladies fuck-off-home' as another theory goes. In fact *golf* doesn't stand for anything, but is instead derived from an old Scottish word for a club or blow, *goulf*, which was in turn probably adopted from Dutch. The earliest reference to *golf* in English comes from an act of the Scottish Parliament passed by James II in 1457, which sought to prohibit it (and football, for that matter) because it distracted Scots militiamen from their archery practice. An even earlier reference to a game called *colf* (which may or may not reveal the game's true continental origins) also comes from an edict that sought to ban it: passed by the Council of Brussels in 1360, the law threatened to punish 'whoever plays ball with a club', with 'a fine of 20 shillings, or [else] his overcoat will be confiscated'.]

●

The first recorded use of the acronym *OMG* dates from 1917.

[On 9 September 1917, at the height of the First World War, Admiral John Arbuthnot Fisher wrote to Winston Churchill, then Minister for Munitions, to say that 'I hear that a new order of Knighthood is on the tapis – O. M. G. (Oh! My! God!) – Shower it on the Admiralty!'. The letter did not come to public notice until it was published in Fisher's memoirs in 1919, and it wasn't until 2011 that the *Oxford English Dictionary* finally credited Fisher with the earliest known record of *OMG*.]

The French equivalent of *LOL* is *MDR*. It stands for *mort de rire*, or 'dead with laughing'.

In Victorian slang, a *gigglemug* was someone who appeared to smile or laugh constantly.

The visual equivalent of a laughingstock is a *gazingstock* – someone who is being stared at by everyone else.

Astronomer is an anagram of 'moon-starer'.

A *moonquake* is an earthquake on the Moon.

People from Wiltshire are known as *moonrakers*.

[According to the eighteenth-century lexicographer Francis Grose, the nickname *moonraker* commemorates 'some Wiltshire rustics', who 'seeing the figure of the moon in a pond attempted to rake it out'. Wiltshire locals today, however, tend to put their own spin on this story by claiming the men were actually trying to reach smuggled barrels of brandy they had earlier sunk in the pond when they were interrupted by revenue officers and feigned stupidity to escape prosecution.]

A *rakehell* is a lascivious, debauched man.

◆

John Milton invented the word *Pandemonium* as the name of the capital of Hell in *Paradise Lost*.

[John Milton's *Pandemonium* is described in *Paradise Lost* (1667) as the 'city and proud seat of Lucifer', a grand palace in the centre of Hell that 'rises, suddenly built out of the Deep'. Milton coined the word from the Greek for 'place of all demons', and in this literal sense – a place of endless wickedness and uproar – *pandemonium* soon slipped into use in English, as in this nineteenth-century description of a Maori haka:

> The whole dance was accompanied by a noise that would have put pandemonium to shame; it sounded like a beating of trays, dogs fighting, gigantic snoring, and a very full, deep bass rumbling in the throat. At times there seemed to be a kind of rhythmic song, interspersed with yells and short, sharp cries of 'Hue, hue!', 'Ha, ha!', 'Pake-ka!' The young women winked and grinned and twisted about beyond what was strictly correct; but they seemed to enjoy the really hard work of the dance most thoroughly.
>
> — *Popular Science Magazine* (1879)

Nowadays *pandemonium* tends only to be used of any place or state of utter confusion or chaos, as in this description of a German gas attack on a First World War trench:

> For a minute, pandemonium reigned in our trench – Tommies adjusting their helmets, bombers running here and there, and men turning out of the dugouts with fixed bayonets, to man the fire step.
>
> — *Over The Top* (1917), Arthur Guy Empey]

◆

Mount Erebus in Antarctica is named after a region of the underworld in Greek mythology.

[At 3,800 m (12,500 ft), Erebus is Antarctica's second highest volcano and the southernmost active volcano on earth. It was discovered on 27 January 1841 by the British naval officer and explorer Sir James Clark Ross (commemorated in the nearby Ross Sea and Ross Ice Shelf), who named it after his ship, the HMS *Erebus*. In turn, Ross's ship was named after the region of the Greek underworld connecting earth and Hades, through which the dead passed immediately after dying.]

♦

Penguin is thought to derive from the Welsh for 'white head'.

[*Penguin* is one of those unassuming words behind which is hidden a surprisingly complicated and unresolved etymology. Confusing things from the outset is the fact that the name *penguin* first referred to the now-extinct great auk of the North Atlantic Ocean. It was the auk's similarity to the birds spotted (and eaten in considerable numbers) by Sir Francis Drake's circumnavigatory expedition in 1577 that led to its name being transported south. As the ship's admiral, Francis Fletcher, recorded in the log book of the *Golden Hind*:

> [20 August 1577] In these Islands we found great reliefe and plenty of good victualls, for infinite were the Numbers of the foule, which the Welsh men name Pengwin[.]

If a Welsh interpretation of the name is correct, then *penguin* is presumably a compound of *pen*, meaning 'head', and *gwyn*, meaning 'white', although it might instead come from the Latin word *pinguis*, meaning 'plump' or 'dense'. As Fletcher went on:

> [Penguins] breed and lodge at land, and in the day tyme goe downe to the sea to feed, being soe fatt that they can but goe, and their

skins cannot be taken from their bodyes without tearing off the flesh, because of their exceeding fatnes.]

♦

25,000 people in Argentina speak Welsh.

[A Welsh colony known as *Y Wladfa* was established in the Chubut province of southern Argentina in 1865. The brainchild of a Welsh nationalist reverend named Dr Michael D. Jones (who envisaged it as a 'Wales beyond Wales'), a ship of 153 Welsh emigrants landed at Peurto Madryn on the Patagonian coast on 27 July. Although the colonists' early years were problematic – they had been promised a landscape similar to south Wales, but landed instead in a semi-arid desert with little fresh water and a susceptibility to flash floods – their settlement flourished, and by the turn of the twentieth century it had expanded as far west as the Andes. Today, some 50,000 Chubut people – roughly one in eleven – have Welsh ancestry.]

♦

The Welsh word for 'cockerel' is *ceiliog* – that's why there's a cockerel on boxes of Kellogg's Corn Flakes.

[While touring America in the 1920s, the acclaimed Welsh harpist Nansi Richards visited the home of the American industrialist and inventor William Kellogg in Michigan. Kellogg and his brother John had recently made their fortune promoting their own brand of healthy breakfast cereals, but were stumped for a new marketing idea. Richards happened to point out that the brothers' surname was remarkably similar to the Welsh word for 'cockerel', *ceiliog*, and the brand's now long-lived logo was born. According to the Kellogg Company, incidentally, the cockerel's official name is 'Cornelius Rooster'.]

♦

Alectryomancy is a form of divination in which a fortune is interpreted from a cockerel pecking grain off the ground.

♦

In English, cockerels say *cock-a-doodle-do*. In French they say *cocorico*. In Icelandic they say *gaggalagó*. In Scots they say *gog-a-ghuidhe-ghaoidhe*.

♦

Leghorn chickens are named after Livorno, Italy. *Jeans* are named after Genoa, Italy. *Denim* is named after Nîmes, France.

♦

Thirty per cent of the English language is derived from French.

♦

In the eighteenth century, *to have gone to Bordeaux* was slang for 'to be drunk on red wine'.

♦

Vinomadefied means 'utterly soaked with wine'.

♦

Whisky derives from a Gaelic word, *uisgebeatha*, meaning 'water of life'.

♦

Vodka means 'little water' in Russian.

◆

The *daiquiri* cocktail is named after the village of Daiquirí in Cuba.

◆

The *Molotov* of 'Molotov cocktail' means 'hammerer' in Russian.

> [When the Soviet Union invaded Finland in the winter of 1939–40 – leading to the so-called Winter War, and Russia's eventual expulsion from the League of Nations – the Soviet Foreign Affairs Minister, Vyacheslav Molotov, repeatedly denied that the Soviets were bombing Finland, and instead claimed that they were dropping relief crates containing food and other supplies. In response, the Finns nicknamed the Russian bombs *Molotov breadbaskets*, and fought back with improvised incendiaries dubbed *Molotov cocktails*, comprising a glass bottle filled with petrol and topped with a rag acting as a makeshift fuse.
>
> Molotov himself was born Vyacheslav Mikhailovich Skryabin in 1890. He adopted his pseudonym from the Russian word for 'hammer', *molot*, after joining the Social Democratic Labour Party in his late teens. He quickly rose through its ranks to become one of the most prominent political figures in Stalinist Russia, infamously putting his name to the Molotov–Ribbentrop Pact which acted as a 'treaty of non-aggression' between Nazi Germany and the Soviet Union in 1939. Stalin, incidentally, was born Josif Vissariónovich Dzhugashvíli in 1879, and took his pseudonym from the Russian word for 'steel', *stal*.]

◆

The end of a hammer opposite the face is called the *peen*.

◆

Ninnyhammer, *funge*, *foppotee* and *sumph* are all old names for fools and nincompoops.

◆

In Ancient Greece, an *idiot* was someone with no interest in politics.

[That there is any kind of connection between idiocy and politics might come as little surprise, but the fact is that in Ancient Athens an *idiotes* was anyone whose life had no connection with any form of public service. This could mean simply that they were a private person who opted to be disengaged from the running of the city (and indeed *idiot* derives from the Greek word for 'private' or 'one's own', *idios*), but more often than not the term implied that the person in question was ignorant, ill-informed or immature, or else a layman or unskilled worker as opposed to the magistrates, scribes, soldiers and other citizens whose work directly connected them with the state.]

◆

Tory derives from an Irish word for 'outlaw'.

[*Tory* first appeared in English in the seventeenth century as another name for a bandit or thief, and is derived from *tóraidhe* or *tóraí*, an Irish word meaning 'outlaw' or 'plunderer'. It first gained its political connotations in 1679 with the introduction of the Exclusion Bill, an act of Parliament that sought to deny the Catholic Duke of York's claim to the English throne – the present king, Charles II, had no children and so his younger brother, the Duke, remained first in line to succeed him. The Exclusionist Whigs who supported the bill disparagingly nicknamed their opponents 'the Tories', and the nickname remained in use even after the anti-Exclusionists had formed a full-blown political party. The bill itself eventually failed to pass through the House of Lords, and the Duke went on to become King James II on Charles's death in 1685.]

Labour is the collective noun for a group of moles.

◆

Duckmole and *mullingong* are old names for the duck-billed platypus.

◆

The plural of *platypus* is *platypodes*. The plural of *octopus* is *octopodes*.

> [According to the *Oxford English Dictionary*, all three possible plurals of *platypus* and *octopus* – *platypuses*, *platypi*, *platypodes*, and *octopuses*, *octopi*, *octopodes* – are acceptable. However, though the *–podes* spellings are described as 'rare' by the *Oxford English Dictionary*, strictly speaking they are the only truly correct forms, as the final *–pus* of *platypus* and *octopus* is a derivative of the Greek for 'foot', *pous*, which should rightly become *podes* in the plural. *Platypi* and *octopi*, which are often considered the 'proper' plurals, are in fact based on the misconception that *platypus* and *octopus* are Latin names rather than Greek. If this were the case, the *–us* endings here would rightly become *–i* in the plural, as they do in words like *alumnus* and *fungus*.]

◆

Octothorp is an alternative name for the hash sign #.

◆

The German name for the @ sign means 'spider monkey'.

> [Although in modern German the @ sign is often called the 'at', it is nevertheless also nicknamed the *Klammeraffe* (literally 'clinging-monkey'), in reference to the @ sign's similarity to the spider monkey's

coiled tail. German is by no means the only language whose speakers have interpreted the @ sign in some surprisingly inventive ways, however: in Italian, @ is *la chiocciola*, or 'the snail'; in Greek it is *papaki*, meaning 'duckling'; in Denmark and Sweden it is the *snabel-a*, or 'elephant's-trunk-A'; and in parts of Finland it is *kissanhäntä*, or 'cat's tail'. Perhaps strangest of all, however, is *zavináč*, the name by which it is known in Czech and Slovak, which is the local name for a pickled rollmop herring.]

♦

@ is the only new character added to the Morse code alphabet since the First World War.

[The @ sign was officially added to the Morse code alphabet in 2004, 160 years after Samuel Morse's first public demonstration of his telegraphic code in 1844. Comprised of an A (·–) and C (–·–·) combined – supposedly an acronym of 'commercial at', but just likely meant to represent a lower case A wrapped inside an upper case C – the introduction of the @ sign allowed users of Morse code to transmit email addresses for the very first time.]

♦

Shrapnel is named after Henry Shrapnel, who invented a type of fragmenting bomb during the Peninsular War.

♦

A *blockbuster* was originally a gigantic RAF bomb capable of destroying an entire block of buildings.

♦

Semtex is named after Semtín in the Czech Republic, where it was invented in 1966.

◆

The Czech word *prozvonit* means 'to call someone's mobile so that they have your phone number', or 'to end a phone call while it's ringing so that the person you rang is obliged to call back'.

◆

Telephone was originally the name of a 'musical telegraph' that used musical notes to relay messages.

[In the early 1820s, a French violinist named Jean-François Sudré devised a system of communication that assigned twenty-one of the commonest letters of the alphabet to three octaves of the seven notes of the musical scale – *do, re, mi, fa, so, la, ti*. Sudré's system allowed words to be spelled out on practically any musical instrument, but in order to communicate across distances he envisaged an enormous foghorn-like device called a *téléphone* that would operate like a 'musical telegraph'. Sudré continued to refine his idea over the years that followed, culminating in his development of a new 'musical language', *Solrésol*, which assigned whole words to combinations of notes to create a rich 9,000-word vocabulary. Although his Solrésol system demanded that those who decoded the messages had impeccable perfect pitch (if interpreted just one note too low, for instance, 'whale' could be misread as 'excrement'), despite their shortcomings, Sudré's ideas earned him considerable acclaim in his lifetime, and he toured much of Europe in the early 1800s demonstrating his work to appreciative – if frugal – audiences:

On Wednesday, the 8th of July, M. Sudré gave a public demonstration of his 'Musical Language', in the Concert Room of the King's Theatre; and in order to fill up a certain quantity of time agreeably, as well as to relieve himself and justify his demand of half a guinea

as the price of admission, several pieces of music were executed by
various performers of eminence.

— *The Musical Library* (1835)]

♦

The first note of the 'do re mi' scale was originally called *ut*.

♦

Cabbaged, *debagged* and *baggage* are the longest words that can be played on a musical instrument.

[The seven musical notes from A to G can be used to spell out more
than a hundred English words, including *decaf*, *acceded*, *babe*, *egged*, *feed-bag* and *gaga*. The use of H in place of B (and B in place of B-flat)
that is popular in some European countries would expand this total to
more than 200, and would add such words as *headache*, *beached*, *chafed*,
egghead and *deadheaded* to the list. This arrangement also allowed the
composer Johann Sebastian Bach to secrete his surname into a number
of his works, and gave several later composers the opportunity to pay
tribute to him in their own compositions – most notably Franz Liszt's
Fantasy and Fugue on the Theme B-A-C-H (1855).]

♦

A *bazooka* was originally a trombone-like musical instrument.

[In a review of the US comedian Bob Burns' show in December 1935,
Newsweek magazine commented that:

Burns peps up his lengthy yarns with periodic outbursts on his
own invention, the bazooka, a trombone-like instrument confec-
ted of two gas-pipes and a whisky funnel.

The review provides the earliest known record of the word *bazooka* in English, and neatly explains Burns' inadvertent contribution to anti-tank warfare: when US soldiers were first issued with the M1 rocket-launcher in June 1942, they apparently noticed its similarity to Burns' bazooka and the nickname stuck.]

♦

The French word for 'paperclip' is *trombone*.

♦

Saxophones are named after their inventor, Adolphe Sax. *Leotards* are named after their inventor, Jules Léotard. *Stetsons* are named after their inventor, John Batterson Stetson.

♦

The *hat trick* was originally a cricketing term, and referred to a player taking three wickets with three balls.

♦

The first film ever marketed as a *threequel* – the follow-up to a sequel – was *Jaws 3-D* in 1983.

♦

A *wobbegong* is a type of Australian carpet shark.

♦

Nothing rhymes with *carpet*.

[This didn't stop one anonymous and ingenious nineteenth-century writer from penning the following poem – entitled 'Lines to a

Pretty Barmaid' – in answer to a challenge in New York's *Knickerbocker* magazine calling on readers to submit a rhyme for the word *carpet*:

> Sweet maid of the inn,
> 'Tis surely no sin
> To toast such a beautiful bar pet.
> Believe me, my dear,
> Your feet would appear
> At home on a nobleman's carpet.]

♦

Nothing rhymes with *orange*.

[*Orange* is probably the most famous unrhymable word in the English language. As a result, it has been the subject of many years' discussion and debate attempting to uncover a rhyme for it, all of which has come up with little more than a collection of near misses, some fairly unusual proper nouns (like the surnames *Dorringe* and *Gorringe*, and *Blorenge*, a hill in the Brecon Beacons), and some equally unusual poetry. If names and other proper nouns are discounted, the only real contender here is *sporange*, an alternative name for the spore capsule or 'sporangium' of a plant, but as this is pronounced with the stress on the second syllable rather than the first ('spuh-*ranj*', not '*spo*-runj') it too fails to fit the brief.

The fact is no English word rhymes with *orange* – but like *carpet*, that didn't stop one intrepid (and sadly also anonymous) nineteenth-century writer from compiling *Uncle, Can You Find A Rhyme For Orange?* (1869), a collection of four-line verses each of which valiantly attempts to contrive a rhyme:

> 'So, gentle nephew, you're returned
> From town without an orange.'
> 'True, my good Uncle, why? nor pound
> My pocket boasted, nor change.']

◆

There was no word for the colour *orange* in English until the sixteenth century.

[Like *Brazil* vs. *Brazil nuts* and *hobby* vs. *hobby-horse* (see page 193), another etymological chicken-and-the-egg problem concerns the word *orange*: the colour, surprisingly, is named after the fruit, not the other way around. Before oranges began to be imported more widely into England from the continent in the 1400s and 1500s, anything orange-coloured had simply to be described in terms of either red or yellow, as in this description of a fox from Chaucer's *Nun's Priest's Tale*:

His colour was bitwixe yelow and reed,
And tipped was his tayl and both his eeris
[*His colour was between yellow and red,
and tipped was his tail and both ears.*]]

◆

***Agent Orange* is colourless. It took its name from the orange stripe painted on the containers it was kept in.**

◆

***Pink* was originally the name of a murky greenish-yellow colour.**

[This use of pink dates back to the mid-1400s, although its exact origin before then is unclear. As a pale red colour, pink dates from the mid-1600s and is thought to derive from the popularity of *Dianthus* flowers, known as 'pinks', in Elizabethan England.]

◆

In Tibetan, 'to give a green answer to a blue question' – *gadrii nombor shulen jongu* – means 'to give an answer that is unrelated to the question'.

◆

Anyone who is *xanthodontic* has yellow teeth.

◆

To *grin* originally meant 'to show your teeth'.

◆

An *eccedentesiast* is someone who fakes a smile.

◆

A *much-faker* is someone who mends umbrellas.

◆

Impluvious means 'utterly soaked with rain'.

◆

Petrichor is the earthy smell left in the air after it rains. It literally means 'the life-blood of rocks'.

◆

Cloud meant 'rock' in Old English.

> [The Old English word from which the Modern English cloud is descended was *clud*, which was variously used to mean 'rock', 'stone', or even 'mountain'; the Anglo-Saxon word for 'cloud', meanwhile, was *wolcen*. Somehow – presumably through the similarity of grey rain-clouds to grey masses of rock or stone – the use of *clud* altered over

time, and the modern word cloud came into existence. *Wolcen* by contrast all but disappeared from the language, but is retained in welkin – an old-fashioned or poetic name for the skies or heavens.]

An *ombrosalgia* is a pain felt only during wet weather.

Nostalgia derives from the Greek word for 'pain': the feeling of homesickness it causes was once a genuine medical condition.

The Portuguese word *saudade* has no English equivalent, but essentially means 'an intense melancholic nostalgia or longing for something lost or missing'.

The *dodo* was named after the Portuguese word for 'fool'.

There was once a species of bird native to Hawaii called the *oo*.

The Hawaiian alphabet only has eight consonants.

United Arab Emirates is comprised entirely of alternating vowels and consonants.

[Excluding proper nouns, the longest English word comprised of alternating vowels and consonants is Shakespeare's *honorificabilitudinitatibus* (see page 92), and most other examples of any length are just as obscure and esoteric: *epicoracohumeral* ('pertaining to a joint between the shoulder blade and the humerus'), *aluminosilicate* ('any mineral containing aluminium, oxygen and silicon'), and *iculanibokola* ('a traditional fork once used during cannibal rituals in Fiji'). All Fijian cannibal cutlery aside, among the more familiar words that fit this category are *degenerative*, *verisimilitude*, *unimaginative* and *unapologetic*.]

♦

Dermatoglyphics, the scientific study of fingerprints, is spelled using fifteen completely different letters.

[A word comprised of a set of entirely different letters is called an *isogram*, and there are more than 35,000 of them in the English language including *troublemaking*, *ambidextrously*, *metalworking*, *unpredictably* and *motherfucking*. *Dermatoglyphics* is one of the four longest, along with *uncopyrightable*, *misconjugatedly* and *hydropneumatics*, the branch of engineering that deals with combinations of gases and liquids. The even longer 17-letter word *subdermatoglyphic* – which would mean something like 'relating to the skin beneath the fingertips' – has the potential to steal the title but has yet to be accepted into any mainstream dictionary.]

♦

The proper name for a fingerprint is a *dactylogram*.

[*Daktylos* is the Greek word for 'finger', and is the root of a number of rare and fairly unusual English words: *dactylonomy* is the proper name for counting on the fingers; a *dactylioglyph* is someone who engraves

the gemstones for rings; the adjective *dactylodeiktous* describes anything
you're pointing at with your finger; and if you're *pachydactylous* then
you have thick, fleshy fingers – the opposite of which is *leptodactylous*.]

♦

Young pterodactyls are called *flaplings*.

♦

Brontosaurus means 'thunder-lizard'.

♦

The oversized, widely scattered drops of rain that
precede a thunderstorm are called *thunder-drops*. It was
coined by Alfred Lord Tennyson in his poem *A Dream of
Fair Women*.

♦

'Husky chips of potato fried with reluctant drops of
oil' is the earliest known description of potato chips. It
comes from Charles Dickens' *A Tale of Two Cities*.

♦

An *ecumenopolis* is a theoretical city covering the entire
surface of a planet.

♦

The line separating the light and dark regions of a planet
is called the *terminator*.

♦

Traffic lights are nicknamed *robots* in South Africa.

♦

Roundabouts were once called *rond-points*.

♦

The currencies of Japan, China and South Korea – the *yen*, *yuan* and *won* – all mean 'round'.

♦

Tycoon is the Japanese word for 'great prince'.

♦

The girl's name *Sarah* means 'princess'.

♦

Girl wasn't originally gender-specific, and could be used of either boys or girls.

> [As odd as it might seem to modern English speakers, in early Middle English *gyrle* meant 'child' or 'youngster', regardless of sex, and it wasn't until the fifteenth century that it began to be used exclusively of young women – so when Geoffrey Chaucer wrote of 'the yonge gerles of the diocise' in his *Canterbury Tales*, he was talking about all 'the young children of the diocese'. *Man* likewise could be used of both men and women in Old English, and didn't come to refer exclusively to males until the eleventh century; the general use of *man* to mean 'human' is retained in words like *manslaughter* and *mankind*.]

♦

Yob is derived from 'boy' spelled backwards.

[*Yob* was first recorded in a 'glossary of the back slang' that was included as an appendix to John Camden Hotten's *Dictionary of Modern Slang, Cant and Vulgar Words* in 1859. Back slang was a popular means of coining new slang words in Victorian England, which saw *pounds* become 'dunops', *cabbage* become 'edgabac', *drunk* become 'kennurd', and *boy* become 'yob'. *Three months* became 'erth sith-noms', described by Hotten as 'a term of imprisonment unfortunately very familiar to the lower orders'.]

♦

The first *hooligans* were gangs of young criminals in London in the late nineteenth century.

[*Hooligan* is thought to be a derivative of the Irish surname Houlihan, and indeed most of the earliest records of the word in English come from Victorian cartoons, music-hall numbers, jokes and stage routines that all portrayed some kind of stereotypically daft or disorderly Irishman and his family. Amongst the most notable are a comic strip, *Hooligans*, that appeared in *Nuggets* magazine, a 'Serio-Comic Budget of Pictures and Stories', in the 1890s; *Miss Hooligan's Christmas Cake*, a Scottish broadside ballad dating from the 1880s about a gigantic cake baked by an Irish cook that makes everyone ill; and *The Hooligans*, an enormously successful music-hall number performed by two noted Irish comedians, Charles Brady and Jim O'Connor, in London in 1892:

> Oh, The Hooligans!
> Oh, The Hooligans!
> Always on the riot,
> Cannot keep them quiet,
> Oh, The Hooligans!

Around the same time, a number of gangs of young criminals and ruffians began operating across the capital, and (presumably partly inspired by the lyrics to Brady and O'Connor's song) began calling themselves 'The Hooligans'. After one of the gangs was found guilty of a murder in Lambeth in August 1898, the name *hooligan* was quickly picked up by the press, who began reporting of an 'avalanche of brutality which, under the name of "Hooliganism" … has cast such a dire slur on the social records of South London'.]

♦

No one knows what *London* means.

[There are several competing theories as to what *London* actually means, but none is entirely without question and the true origin of the name remains a mystery. Amongst the least likely is the idea that it derives from *Luna din*, an old Roman-influenced name meaning something like 'moon-fortress'. A more plausible theory is that it's a Welsh word, and might mean something like 'river-fort' (*llyn-din*), or 'pool by the river' (*llyn-dain*). Perhaps the most likely suggestion, however, is that of Professor Richard Coates, an acclaimed professor of place name origins and director of The English Place-Name Society, who suggests that the name might originally have been *Plowonidā*, an ancient word meaning 'boat-river' or 'swimming-river' – namely the point in the course of the Thames where it is no longer possible to cross on foot or horseback.]

♦

The original *no-man's-land* was an unowned area of scrubland in north London that was used for executions.

♦

The guillotine is named after a French doctor called Joseph-Ignace Guillotin.

[For the invention of the guillotine, Dr Joseph-Ignace Guillotin is often presumed to have been a brutal, bloodthirsty militant who was so determined that heads should roll during the French Revolution that he designed a machine to do it as swiftly as possible. In fact, he was nothing of the sort. In fact, he opposed the death penalty. And in fact, he didn't even invent the guillotine. Instead, it was the brainchild of another eighteenth-century French physician, Antoine Louis, who, alongside a German harpsichord manufacturer named Tobias Schmidt, produced such a successful prototype device for lopping off heads that in its early days the guillotine was known as the *louisette*. Dr Guillotin, meanwhile, was merely employed on a committee that sought to reform executions in France, and having determined that decapitation (and, for that matter, as swift a decapitation as possible) was the most humane means of killing someone, Guillotin advocated Louis' invention to the committee on 1 December 1789, claiming that 'with my machine, I can cut the head off in a blink of an eye, with no suffering'.]

Decimation was a Roman punishment in which one in every ten men was put to death. In *vigesimation* it was one in twenty.

A *pennyweight* is ½₀ of an ounce. It was originally the weight of one silver penny.

The *quick* of *quicksilver* means 'living', not 'fast'.

[The use of *quick* to mean 'fast' or 'mobile' first began to appear in English texts in the early 1300s. Before then, the Old English word *cwice* had meant 'living' or 'endowed with life', and it is this earlier sense that is found in a handful of *quick-* words that date from the same period, including *quicksilver*, *quicksand*, *quickset* and *quickening*, an old name for the earliest stage in a pregnancy when foetal movements can be felt. The earliest written record of *quicksilver* comes from an

Anglo-Saxon *Leechbook* (medical textbook) dating from the ninth century, which offers the following advice for treating stomach-ache:

> Wiþ magan wærce: rudan sæd & cwic seolfor & eced bergen
> on neaht nestig. Eft, gnid on eced & on wæter polleian. Sele
> drincan. Sona þæt sar toght.
> [*With pain of stomach: take rue seed and quicksilver and vinegar after a
> night's fasting. Afterwards, grind in vinegar and pennyroyal. Give to
> drink. Soon the soreness will go away.*]

Given that the ingestion of mercury can cause neurological problems, visual impairment, peeling skin and kidney failure, it's unlikely that this remedy ever worked, but at least the patient wouldn't be worrying about his stomach-ache anymore. Other equally ghastly treatments from the same volume include rubbing a mixture of child's urine and honey into the eyes to cure blindness; dripping hot pigeon blood or breast milk on to the eyes to cure conjunctivitis; and placing the boiled eyes of a live crab against the neck to cure 'swollen eyes'. Perhaps strangest of all, however, is this cure for insanity:

> Wiþ þon þe mon sie monaþ-seoc: nim mere swines fel. Wyrc to
> swipan. Swing mid þone man. Sona bið sel. Amen.
> [*In case a man is a lunatic: take the skin of a dolphin. Make it into a
> whip. Swinge him with it. Soon he will be well. Amen.*]]

♦

A *jehu* is a recklessly fast driver, named after one of the Old Testament Kings of Israel, who 'driveth furiously' according to the Bible.

♦

The phrase *eat, drink and be merry* comes from the Old Testament Book of Ecclesiastes.

William Tyndale's Bible (1525) provides the earliest known records of the words *busybody*, *long-suffering*, *broken-hearted*, *castaway* and *scapegoat*.

◆

Tragedy derives from the Greek for 'goat-song'.

> [*Tragedy* is thought to be a derivative of the Greek words *tragos*, meaning 'he-goat', and *oide*, meaning 'ode' or 'song'. The image here is probably that of actors in Ancient Greek tragedies dressing in animal furs and skins in order to play the satyrs and other mythical creatures of Greek folklore, but there are numerous competing theories and etymologies. Incidentally, *tragos* is also the root of *tragus*, the small fleshy protuberance that covers the earhole, which took its name from the soft white hairs that grow on it, and which apparently resemble a goat's beard.]

◆

A *geep* is a cross between a goat and a sheep.

◆

In French, a *mouton enragé* – a 'mad sheep' – is an easy-going person who becomes suddenly and uncharacteristically angry.

◆

In Japanese, sheep say *mee* not *baa*.

◆

The *morepork*, *whippoorwill*, *chiffchaff* and *hoopoe* are all birds named after their calls.

[Found across Europe, Asia and Africa, hoopoes are striking bright orange birds with broad black-and-white-striped wings, curved beaks, and remarkable feathered crests on their heads. Their call – a peculiar cuckoo-like whooping sound – is the origin of not just their common name but of their Latin name, *Upupa epops*, and several other dialect nicknames like *whoophooper*, *hupelot* and *whoopcat*.

Unsurprisingly for such distinctive birds, hoopoes have been a popular subject of myths and folklore in many different cultures over thousands of years. The Egyptians considered them sacred, and used images of hoopoes to decorate the inside of tombs and temples. The Romans considered them an ill omen, and believed that they ate excrement and dead bodies (a belief apparently based on nothing more than their supposed habit of nesting in cemeteries). And one mediaeval French bestiary describes how young hoopoes supposedly tend for their elder relatives, licking the blindness from their eyes and plucking out old feathers so that new ones can grow in their place. The hoopoe's extraordinary appearance has also led to them being traditionally considered clownish or gullible creatures – in fact, the word *dupe* is thought to derive from the French *de huppe*, meaning 'of the hoopoe'.]

♦

Onomatopoeia literally means 'making names'.

♦

Some words that are presumed to have originally been onomatopoeic: *rook*, *pebble*, *kite*, *laugh* and *owl*.

♦

To take owls to Athens was the Roman equivalent of 'to take coals to Newcastle'.

Archipelago was originally just another name for the Aegean Sea. The Aegean contains so many islands it eventually came to refer to any island chain or group.

♦

Serendipity derives from an old name for Sri Lanka.

> [*Serendip* is thought to be a corruption of a Sanskrit name meaning 'land of lions'. The derivative *serendipity* was coined by the English writer Horace Walpole, who in a letter in 1754 explained that he had based the word on an old Persian story called *The Princes of Serendip*, the title characters of which he explained were 'always making discoveries, by accidents and sagacity, of things they were not in quest of'.]

♦

Insulin derives from the Latin word for 'island'.

> [The Latin word for 'island' is *insula*, from which is derived a whole host of words including *peninsula* (literally 'almost an island'), *insulate* (literally 'to make into an island'), and *insulin*, so-called as it is manufactured by the pancreas in a series of components known as 'the islets of Langerhans'.]

♦

Diabetes was once called *pissing evil*.

♦

In Finland, a *poronkusema* is the distance a reindeer can travel without stopping to urinate – roughly four and a half miles.

In the Middle Ages, ants were known as *pismires* because the acid they secrete smells like urine.

◆

Accra in Ghana means 'ants'. *Abidjan* in Côte d'Ivoire means 'the leaves'. *Zimbabwe* means 'houses of stones'.

◆

To *lapidate* means 'to stone to death'.

◆

A *chelidonius* is a stone taken from the gizzard of a swallow that was once supposed by to have magical healing powers.

◆

A *quarantine* was once the length of time a widow was permitted to remain in her deceased husband's home.

> [*Quarantine* is a derivative of the Latin word for 'forty', *quadraginta*, and originally referred to the forty days Jesus spent fasting in the desert. Based on this original meaning, in the Middle Ages widows were given a forty-day *quarantine* in which to vacate their husbands' homes, and a medical *quarantine* was originally the forty-day period in which ships would be held out of port in Venice until they could be proven to be free of the plague.]

◆

Widower is thought to be the only English word whose male form is longer than the female equivalent.

> [Excluding compound words (like _bridegroom_) and pairs of words derived from unrelated roots (like _husband_/_wife_ and _cock_/_hen_), ordinarily in English the female equivalent of a pair of male/female words tends either to take a longer suffix than its male counterpart (as in _aviator_/_aviatrix_), or else is formed by adding a female suffix to a male root (as in _actor_/_actress_ or _hero_/_heroine_). _Widow_/_widower_ uniquely bucks this trend by adding its suffix to the male equivalent, making it the longer of the two.
>
> _Widow_ was originally gender-neutral and so could be used of either a man or a woman who had outlived their spouse, but over time it came to be used exclusively of women, likely for no other reason than the fact that women tend to outlive men (and men were more likely to be killed in battle or assassinated in office, etc.). This, however, left a gap in the language for a male equivalent of _widow_, which was finally filled in the mid-1300s when the inflected form _widower_ first began to be used.]

♦

A female lobster is called a _hen_.

♦

Someone _as fussy as a hen with one chick_ is unnecessarily particular about trivial matters.

♦

Pecking orders derive from the hierarchical behaviour of chickens.

♦

A *hencackle* is a trivial concern or inconsequential event.

♦

Eggs were once called *cackle-berries* in American slang.

♦

In the eighteenth century, *big gooseberry season* was the time of year when Parliament wasn't in session and newspapers had little to report on besides trivial matters.

> [In the explanation of this term in his *Dictionary of Phrase and Fable* (1898), the English lexicographer Ebenezer Cobham Brewer stated that, 'It is at such times that newspapers are glad of any subject to fill their columns and amuse their readers; monster gooseberries will do for such a purpose'.]

♦

Gossamer means 'goose-summer', probably in reference to the similarity of gossamer to goose down.

♦

Summer fever and *summer catarrh* are old names for hay fever.

> [Hay fever has been known by a variety of different names over time, including *rose fever* or *rose cold*, *hay-asthma*, *rye asthma* and *pollen fever*. *Hay fever* was coined in an article in a medical journal in 1829.]

♦

Ephemeral derives from the Latin phrase *ephemera febris*, meaning 'one-day fever'.

The sixth, eighth, tenth and twelfth day of a disease – and every day ending in a two, six, eight or zero after that – were once known as the *medicinal days*, on which treatments could be administered most safely.

[The idea that certain days in the course of an illness have different implications is an ancient one, mainly associated today with the ideas of Greek physician Hippocrates. A cornerstone of Hippocratic medicine were the so-called *critical*, *judicial* and *medicinal days*: the first, eighth, fifteenth and twenty-second days of an illness (after which it was classified as 'chronic') were the *critical* days, on which a patient was either expected to make a recovery or take a turn for the worse (which was, incidentally, the original *crisis* point). The first *judicial day* was the third day, on which the full scope of an illness could be assessed, after which any future judicial days would fall directly between the critical days. And the *medicinal days* were those that were neither critical nor judicial, and so when treatment could be administered safely.]

◆

Hoplochrism is a superstitious form of medicine in which the weapon that causes a wound is treated instead of the wound itself.

◆

Abracadabra was once believed to have genuine magical powers.

[No one is quite sure where the word *abracadabra* comes from, nor precisely what it is supposed to mean. Its supposed healing abilities, however, have been discussed and debated in medical textbooks dating as far back as the third century, when the Roman physician Serenus

Sammonicus explained the following treatment – apparently based on an even earlier Greek method – for curing malaria:

> Write on a paper the word ABRACADABRA, repeat it several times under the other taking out the letter at the extremity of the word until, as more and more letters are taken out, only one is left and that you see is in the form of a narrow cone.

This triangle of letters should then be worn as an amulet around the neck, and – as if by magic – the malaria will be cured.]

♦

One possible origin of *hocus-pocus* is that it's a corruption of 'Hoc est corpus meum' – words from the Latin Catholic Mass.

♦

A *zombie* was originally the part of a person's soul that could be removed and bottled using voodoo magic.

♦

A *punt* is the dint in the bottom of a wine bottle.

♦

A *bunt* is the middlemost part of a sail that billows out in the wind.

♦

Opportunity is derived from the Latin for 'towards a harbour', and originally referred to the winds that help a ship into port.

To jibber the kibber was a seventeenth-century phrase meaning to deliberately cause a shipwreck by giving misleading signals from the land.

◆

The adjective *naufragous* describes anything that causes a shipwreck.

◆

Iceberg means 'island-mountain'.

◆

The Tibetan name for Mount Everest, *Qomolangma*, means 'holy mother'.

◆

Kathmandu means 'wooden temple' in Nepali.

◆

A cross between a Himalayan yak and a domestic cow is a *dzho*.

◆

A group of buffalo is called an *obstinacy*.

◆

Jusqu'auboutism is the policy of doggedly seeing something through to the very end.

[*Jusqu'au bout* is essentially the French equivalent of 'to the bitter end', and implies something being doggedly taken all the way through to its conclusion. It first began to appear in English in reference to the First World War, with George Bernard Shaw writing in 1918 that 'in Constantinople it will be a matter of fighting *jusqu'au bout*', and Aldous Huxley referring to himself as a *jusquauboutiste* in reference to the war in France. *Jusquauboutism* first appeared in a wartime newspaper report describing 'extreme German jusqu'auboutisme' in 1917.]

Intransigence is a palindrome in Morse code.

[Meaning 'stubbornness' or 'obstinacy', the 13-letter word *intransigence* is spelled [·· ·· - ··· ·· - ··· ·· ··· · ·· ····· ·] in Morse code. Although the letters themselves don't read the same backwards as forwards, its pattern of dots and dashes do, making it one of the longest known palindromes in Morse code. Equally lengthy examples include *sopranos* [··· --- ···· ··· ·· ·· --- ···], *bottommost* [···· --- - - --- -- -- --- ··· -], *interpreted* [·· ·· - · ··· ···· ··· · · · ···], *protectorate* [···· ··· --- · · ···· · --- ··· ·· · ·] and *endomitotic* [· ·· ··· --- -- ·· - ···· - ·· ····], a biological term referring to the division of chromosomes inside a nucleus. The longest word comprised entirely of dots, incidentally, is *sissies* [··· ·· ··· ··· ·· · ···], while the longest made of dashes is either *tom-tom* [- --- -- - --- --] or *motmot* [-- --- - -- --- -], a colourful Latin American bird.]

An *emordnilap* is a word that spells another when it is reversed – like 'pots' and 'stop', or 'pets' and 'step'.

An *ananym* is a word coined by reversing the letters of another – so the *ohm* is a unit of resistance, while the *mho* is a unit of conductance.

[Ananyms – like *mho*, *yrneh* (see below) and *yob* – are fairly scarce in standard English, with the vast majority of known examples tending to be slang or colloquial expressions, fictional inventions (like Samuel Butler's *Erewhon* or Dylan Thomas's Llareggub, the setting of *Under Milk Wood*), place names (there are towns called Adanac and Saxet in Canada and Texas, respectively), or trade names (like Oprah Winfrey's *Harpo* corporation). Elsewhere, the old Scots name *Segna* is often said to be derived from 'Agnes' spelled backwards, and besides the *mho* and *yrneh*, the *therblig* is a unit used in time-and-motion studies invented by the American engineer and theorist Frank Bunker Gilbreth.]

♦

The *yrneh* is a unit of inverse electrical inductance. It was coined by reversing the letters of 'henry', the unit of electrical inductance named after the American physicist Joseph Henry.

♦

Shakespeare's *Henry IV: Part 1* contains the earliest recorded use of the words *upstairs* and *downstairs*.

♦

The *wellhole* is the open space in a floor filled by a staircase.

[This space is often referred to as the *stairwell*, but strictly speaking that refers to the space or shaft *between* the floors of a building that is filled by a staircase. Confusingly, this shaft can also be called the *wellhole*, as can any opening between the floors of a building such as that filled by a chimneystack, or one deliberately left open to let sunlight shine down from one floor to another.]

♦

To *thrill* originally meant 'to pierce a hole'. Your *nostrils* were originally your 'nose-thrills'.

♦

To *reek* originally meant 'to give off smoke'. It didn't come to mean 'to smell' until the 1700s.

♦

Funk was originally a seventeenth-century word for the stale smell of tobacco smoke.

♦

Nicotine is named after Jean Nicot, a sixteenth-century French ambassador who promoted the medicinal use of tobacco.

♦

Camouflage is derived from a French word meaning 'to blow smoke in someone's face'.

♦

A *wafture* is anything able to be wafted.

♦

Malaria means 'bad air' in Italian. It was once thought to be caused by the smell of stagnant swamps.

♦

William Wordsworth was *anosmic* – he had no sense of smell. Charles Dickens was *chiroptophobic* – he was afraid

of bats. Salvador Dalí was *acridophobic* – he was scared
of grasshoppers.

◆

The phrase *knee-high to a grasshopper* was originally
'knee-high to a toad'.

> [The earliest record of anything being *knee-high* comes from an
> eighteenth-century horticultural guidebook, *The Modern Husbandman*,
> compiled by the English agriculturalist William Ellis in 1744. In it, Ellis
> describes a crop of 'cole-seed' (oilseed rape) planted in mud dredged
> from the bottom of a pond that 'by Michaelmas following … [was]
> knee-high, and served as an excellent alternate food for turkies'. It
> wasn't until the early 1800s that *knee-high* began appearing in various
> standardised sayings, the earliest of which, 'knee-high to a toad', dates
> from 1814. It was quickly followed by 'knee-high to a mosquitoe' in
> (1824), then 'a frog' (1833), 'a bumbly-bee' (1833), 'a splinter' (1841) and
> finally 'grasshopper' in 1851.]

◆

Brekekekex is the sound of croaking frogs.

> [In English, frogs *croak*, or *ribbit*. In Japanese, they *kero*. In German,
> confusingly, they *quak*. And in Ancient Greek, they *brekekekex*. Coined
> by Aristophanes in his play *The Frogs* in 405 BC, *brekekekex* forms part
> of a refrain repeated by a chorus of talking frogs who accompany the
> god Dionysus as he rows across a lake on the way to Hades to resur-
> rect the playwright Euripides. The Greeks, it seems, weren't big fans
> of realism.

>> *Brekekekex, ko-ax, ko-ax!*
>> *Brekekekex, ko-ax, ko-ax!*
>> We children of the spring and lake
>> Let us wake our full choir-shout,

As all the flutes are ringing out,
Our symphony of clear-voiced song.]

♦

The old English dialect word *spanghew* means 'to toss a frog into the air using a stick'.

[In a 'glossary of old and original words made use of in common conversation in the north of England' published in 1780, the English writer John Hutton defined *spanghewing* as:

[…] a cruel custom amongst lads of blowing up a frog by inserting a straw under the skin at the anus; the inflated frog was then jerked into the middle of the pond by being put on a cross stick, the other end being struck, so that the frog jumped high into the air.

According to the *English Dialect Dictionary*, this nasty game was once known across a stretch of Britain extending south from Scotland as far as Cheshire, Oxfordshire and Lincolnshire. Happily *spanghewing* has long disappeared, and nowadays tends only to be defined as 'to throw into the air'.]

♦

Halomancy is a form of divination that involves reading a fortune from salt thrown into the air.

♦

Salad means 'salted'.

[*Salad* is derived from *herba salata*, literally meaning 'salted herbs' or 'salted vegetables' in Latin. It is supposed to have been a popular dish in Ancient Rome.]

♦

Wortsalat, or 'word salad', is jumbled speech and disorderly writing.

◆

In the eighteenth century, an incoherent clergyman who stumbled over his words was a *puzzle-text*.

◆

The first ever crossword puzzle was called a *word-cross*.

> [The earliest crossword puzzle was a diamond-shaped 'word-cross' that appeared in *New York World* magazine on 21 December 1913. Compiled by a British-born journalist named Arthur Wynne, the word-cross contained thirty-two symmetrically-arranged words of three to seven letters each, with a series of straightforward word-association clues listed below. The first crossword clue was 'what bargain hunters enjoy'; the first answer was 'sales'.]

◆

A cross between a blackberry and a raspberry is a *loganberry*.

◆

The Swedish word for 'wild-strawberry patch', *smultronställe*, is used of any idyllic place or refuge.

◆

Baccalaureate derives from the Latin for 'laurel-berry'. It originally referred to laurel wreaths bestowed on victors.

◆

The infinity sign, ∞, is called the *lemniscate*. Its name means 'decorated with ribbons' in Latin.

> [The use of the symbol ∞ to represent infinity dates back to 1655, when the English mathematician (and chief code-breaker of the English Parliament) John Wallis used it in his geometric textbook *Tractatus de Sectionibus Conicis*, 'A Tract on Conic Sections'. Where Wallis himself took the symbol from is unclear, although various theories suggest it could be a corruption of a lower case omega, ω, the last letter of the Greek alphabet, or else a variation of CIƆ, an old version of the Roman numeral for 1,000.]

No one knows where the dollar sign, $, comes from.

> [There are numerous different theories claiming to account for the dollar sign, the most likely of which is that it developed in the late 1700s from an overlapping P and S, probably derived from the *peso* or 'Spanish dollar' that was once widely used in Spanish American colonies. Alternatively, $ could be a corrupted image of the Pillars of Hercules that appear on the Spanish coat of arms; a combination of a slash (/) and an 8, representing the original 'pieces of eight'; or else an overlapping 'PTSI', the hallmark of the Spanish mint at Potosí in Bolivia, which dates back as far as the sixteenth century.]

Dollar derives from *joachimstaler*, the name of a sixteenth-century coin made from silver mined in Joachimstal, a Czech spa town.

Spas are named after the Belgian town of Spa. *Duffel coats* are named after the Belgian town of Duffel.

Netherlands means 'lower lands'. *Holland* means 'woodland'. *Dutch* means 'German'.

◆

The Luxembourgish word for 'turkey', *Schnuddelhong*, means 'snot-hen'.

◆

The Turkish word for 'turkey', *hindi*, means 'Indian'. The Portuguese word for 'turkey' is *peru*. The Malay word for 'turkey', *ayam belanda*, means 'Dutch chicken'.

[The full origin of the name *turkey* is even more confusing than this geographical mishmash of names might suggest. In Tudor England, the name *turkey* was originally given to the African guinea fowl, so-called as it was imported into Europe via Turkey. (Confusing things even more, the name *turkey-cock* was also used of peacocks in the 1500s, but we'll leave that be.) Around the same time, Spanish colonists in the New World began exporting North American turkeys to Europe, and as simply another large and rather odd-looking bird that tasted delicious, European diners began referring to it as the *turkey* as well. But it's not just English speakers who mixed up the two birds, nor who botched up their geography – the Italians (*pollo d'India*), French (*dinde*), Polish (*indyk*), Russians (*indeyka*) and Turks (*hindi*) all named their turkeys after India, which was wrongly presumed to be the New World; the Dutch (*kalkoen*), Danes (*kalkun*), Lithuanians (*kalakutas*) and Finns (*kalkkuna*) were all even more specific (and all misguidedly incorrect) when they named their turkeys after Calicut, a port on India's Malabar coast; the Portuguese (*peru*) named their turkey after Peru, which had been conquered by Pizarro around the same time turkeys began appearing on European dining tables; and the Malayans named it the

'Dutch chicken', after the colonists who introduced the birds to the Dutch East Indies in the 1600s.]

♦

The Hindi equivalent of 'it's no use crying over spilt milk' – *ab pachhtaaye hote kya, jab chidiya chug gayi khet?* – means 'what's the point of crying when the birds ate the whole farm?'

♦

The Russian equivalent of 'easier said than done' – *blizok lokotok, da ne ukusish* – means 'your elbow is close, but you can't bite it'.

♦

In the eighteenth century, an *elbow-shaker* was a habitual gambler.

♦

Shakespeare was the first writer to use *elbow* to mean 'to jostle out of the way'.

♦

The proper name for the point of your elbow is the *olecranon*. The proper name for the back of your hand is the *opisthenar*.

♦

A *main-de-gloire*, or 'hand of glory', is a lucky charm made from the severed and preserved hand of an executed criminal.

♦

In Victorian slang, a *masterpiece of nightwork* was a strikingly handsome or beautiful criminal.

♦

To *elucubrate* means 'to work by lamplight'.

♦

The lights or stars you see when you tightly close or rub your eyes are called *phosphenes*.

> [Derived from the Greek for 'to reveal lights', *phosphenes* were first described in the early 1800s. They're usually caused by a temporary increase in pressure inside the eyeball – such as that caused by rubbing the eye – which stimulates the cells of the retina automatically, giving the appearance of lights when there is no light actually present.]

♦

Babes-in-the-eyes are the tiny reflections of yourself that you can see in the eyes of another person.

♦

In the early 1900s, *misplaced eyebrow* was a nickname for a moustache.

♦

The flat, bare part of the forehead between the eyebrows is called the *glabella*.

◆

The Latin word for 'eyebrow', *supercilium*, is the origin of *supercilious* – as supercilious people frequently raise their eyebrows.

◆

The aural equivalent of an *eyesore* is an *earsore* – an unpleasant sound or cacophonous noise.

◆

The little finger is also known as the *auricular*, or 'ear-finger'.

> [So-called because it's the best-sized finger for poking in your ear, the smallest finger of the hand has been known as the *auricular* or 'ear-finger' since mediaeval times, with its earliest record found in a grammatical textbook written at the turn of the eleventh century. Although nowadays it's largely been superseded by *little finger* or *pinkie* (a Scots nickname dating from the early 1800s), the name *auricular* lives on in a handful of English dialects as well as in the French name *doigt auriculaire*.]

◆

The part of your ear that contains the wax is called the *alveary*. It's also another name for a beehive.

◆

Melissa means 'honeybee' in Greek.

◆

Dumbledore is an old name for a bumblebee.

> [*Dor* was a general name in Old English for any large flying or buzzing insect, and it's been variously applied to different species of fly, beetle, bee and hornet ever since. *Dumbledore* dates from the eighteenth century when it was first listed in *A Provincial Glossary* (1787) of English dialect terms and localisms, although an even earlier form, *drumble-bee*, dates back to the Tudor period. Nowadays, it's irretrievably attached to the character of Professor Albus Dumbledore in J. K. Rowling's Harry Potter books: Rowling apparently chose the name in allusion to the professor's love of music, as she 'imagined him walking around humming to himself' like a bumblebee.]

◆

In Middle English, *muggle* was another name for a fish's tail.

◆

In Tudor England, *fishmonger's daughter* was a euphemism for a prostitute.

◆

The opposite of a euphemism is a *dysphemism* – an insult or an unpleasant turn of phrase used in place of a nicer one.

◆

Innuendo means 'by nodding' in Latin.

◆

There are no words for *yes* and *no* in Latin.

[Latin is actually one of a handful of languages with no precise equivalents of *yes* and *no*. In their place are a system of so-called 'sentence adverbs' like *certe* ('certainly'), *nimirum* ('without doubt'), *sane* ('indeed', 'truly') and *minime* ('not at all'), which can all be used to indicate either agreement or disagreement. Latin speakers also employed a clever technique known as echo response, in which part of a preceding question would be repeated to show a person's response – e.g. 'Are you going?' / 'Going!'.]

♦

There is no Q in the names of any states of the USA.

[In fact, Q is the only letter of the alphabet absent from a full list of the United States: J appears in New Jersey, X in both Texas and New Mexico, and Z in Arizona. Likewise, there is no Q or Z in the names of the US state capitals: there are Js in Jackson (Mississippi), Jefferson City (Missouri) and Juneau (Alaska), and an X in Phoenix (Arizona). Incidentally, Pierre, the capital of South Dakota, is the only state capital that does not share a single letter with its corresponding state.]

♦

Ventriloquism contains every letter of the alphabet from Q to V.

[Excluding exceptionally long and uncommon technical terms, no English word has yet been found that contains more than eight consecutive letters of the alphabet somewhere inside it. What makes the chain of letters in *VenTRiloQUiSm* (and its derivatives) so exceptional, however, is it contains two of the least frequently used letters of the alphabet, Q and V. Other six-letter chains are found in *feedback* (ABCDEF), *kleptomania* (KLMNOP) and *liverwurst* (RSTUVW); a seven-letter series appears in *lightfaced* (CDEFGHI); and an apparently

♦

Engastrimyth is another name for a ventriloquist. Both
words mean 'stomach-speaker'.

♦

The proper name for stomach rumbles is *borborygmi*.

♦

In Tudor England, *to fish out of the bottom of your stomach*
meant 'to divulge your biggest secret'.

♦

Angledog, *clap-bait*, *gilt-tail* and *cow-turd-bob* are all words
for a worm or grub used as fishing bait.

♦

An *amnicolist* is anyone who lives beside a river.

♦

Spear fishing is also known as *weequashing*.

[*Weequash* is derived from *wigwas*, an Algonquin word meaning 'birch-
bark', and it seems likely that it would originally have referred to a
birchwood torch used by Native Americans while hunting after dark.
The name eventually came to apply to any hunting or fishing trip carried out by torchlight, as in this description taken from a letter written
by a Massachusetts resident in 1792:

Great Neck in Mashpee [sixty miles south of Boston] is a place famous for eels. The Indians, when they go in a canoe with a torch, to catch eels in the night, call it Weequash, or anglicised, *weequashing*.]

◆

Sir Walter Scott invented the word *freelance*.

[The *free* of *freelance* doesn't mean 'without payment' (although modern-day freelancers might like to disagree), but rather 'unrestricted' or 'uninhibited', and it originally referred to a mediaeval knight who would offer his services to any side in return for cash. The word first appeared in Sir Walter Scott's *Ivanhoe* (1819):

I offered Richard the service of my Free Lances, and he refused them – I will lead them to Hull … and embark for Flanders; thanks to the bustling times, a man of action will always find employment.

Before then, *freelancers* like this had been known as *free-companions*, members of a so-called 'free company' of mercenaries without any allegiance to a particular side.]

◆

The Scots word *tartle* refers to the awkward hesitation of having to introduce someone whose name you can't remember.

◆

Onomatomania is the annoyance of not being able to come up with the right word at the right time.

◆

Word is the 487th commonest word in the English language.

♦

Time is the commonest noun in the English language.

> [Elsewhere, *man* is ranked as the seventh-commonest noun, ahead of *woman* in fourteenth place; the most frequently encountered part of the body is *hand*, in tenth place, followed by *eye* in thirteenth; and *year*, the third-commonest noun, is followed by *day* in fifth place, *week* in seventeenth, and *month* in fortieth. *Time*, incidentally, is the fifty-fifth most frequently used word in the entire English language.]

♦

O'clock is an abbreviation of 'of the clock'.

♦

Grandfather clocks take their name from a Victorian song called 'My Grandfather's Clock'.

> [Grandfather clocks are properly known as 'long-case' or 'pendulum' clocks – although in the early 1800s they were also nicknamed *wag-at-the-walls*. Their more familiar name comes from a popular ballad written by the American composer Henry Clay Work in 1876:
>
> > My grandfather's clock was too large for the shelf,
> > So it stood ninety years on the floor.
> > It was taller by half than the old man himself,
> > Though it weighed not a pennyweight more.
>
> The song was published in sheet music booklets featuring an image of a long-case clock on the cover, and its huge popularity in the late 1800s no doubt helped to establish *grandfather clock* as the long-case clock's more preferred name.]

Your *quatrayle* is your father's grandfather's grandfather – or your great-great-great-grandfather.

♦

Your *siblings* are your brothers and sisters. Your *niblings* are your nieces and nephews.

♦

Googol – a one followed by one hundred zeros – was coined by the nephew of US mathematician Edward Kasner.

♦

A *googolplex* is one followed by a googol of zeros. A *googolplexian* is one followed by a googolplex of zeros.

♦

A *zenzizenzizenzic* is a number raised to its eighth power.

[In the Middle Ages square numbers were also known as *zenzics*, derived from a German spelling of the Italian word *censo*, meaning 'squared'. Based on this, English mathematicians in the sixteenth and seventeenth centuries could talk of *zenzicubes* ('the cube of a square number'), *zenzicubicubes* ('the square of a cube number cubed'), and *zenzizenzizenzics* ('the square of a square of a square'), all of which were coined by the Welsh mathematician Robert Recorde in his grand arithmetical textbook *The Whetstone of Witte* (1557). A *zenzizenzizenzic* is ultimately a number raised to eighth power, or $((x^2)^2)^2$ – so 256 is the zenzizenzizenzic of two.]

A *multiplicand* is the number that is multiplied by a multiplier.

> [All of the values and results involved in basic mathematical calculations have their own names. In $2 \times 3 = 6$, 2 is the *multiplicand*, 3 is the *multiplier*, and the result, 6, is called the *product*. Oppositely, in $6 \div 3 = 2$, 6 is the *dividend*, 3 is the *divider*, and 2 is the *quotient*. In $2 + 4 = 6$, 2 is the *augend*, 4 is the *addend*, and 6 is the *sum*, and in $6 - 4 = 2$, 6 is the *minuend*, 4 is the *subtrahend*, and the result is called the *difference*.]

Tantuple is another name for a square number – a number multiplied by itself.

An arrangement of five things in a square with one in the centre – like the five on a die – is called a *quincunx*.

A *quinqueliteral* word has five letters.

Of the hundred commonest English words, only *people* and *because* have more than five letters.

> [The commonest words in most languages are typically functional words like prepositions (*with*, *on*), conjunctions (*and*, *but*) and pronouns (*I*, *you*). Their frequency has largely helped to keep them short and simple, and often monosyllabic – indeed twenty of the hundred commonest words in English have only two letters. *People*,

incidentally, is the sixty-first most common word in English, while *because* is ninety-fourth.]

◆

In Morse code, all the numbers from zero to nine have five characters.

[No letter in the Morse code alphabet is comprised of more than four dots and dashes, but the alphabet as a whole follows no strict pattern other than keeping the most frequent letters as short as possible (E is a single dot ·, T is a single dash -), while less common letters are more complicated (J is ·---, Q is --·-). Numbers, however, follow a much more predictable pattern based around a symmetrical series of dots and dashes that always total five: one is a single dot followed by four dashes [·----]; two is a pair of dots followed by three dashes [··---]; three is three dots [···--], and so on up to five [·····], after which the pattern reverses and six becomes a single dash followed by four dots [-····]; seven is two dashes and three dots [--···], and so on up to five consecutive dashes [-----], which represents zero.]

◆

No English word contains any more than six consecutive consonants – as in *watchstrap* or *catchphrase*.

[*Rhythms* is usually said to be the longest English word without an A, E, I, O or U, although some dictionaries list the even longer *symphysy*, meaning 'a fusion', or 'a joining of two parts'. Both of these however utilise the letter Y as if it were a vowel, as do other famously vowel-less words like *lynx*, *crypt* and *syzygy*, an astronomical term referring to an alignment of three celestial bodies. If Ys are excluded, no word in English apparently tolerates any more than six consecutive consonants, like those seen in *watchstrap*, *catchphrase*, *latchstring*, *flightstrip*, *sightscreen* and *bergschrund*, a glacial crevasse.]

Dominoes with seven spots – like 1/6 and 3/4 – are called *matadors*.

♦

The proper name for a bullfight is a *tauromachy*.

♦

Bully is derived from the Dutch word for 'brother', and was originally a term of endearment.

[It's common for the meanings of words to change over time, but the change seen in *bully* is perhaps one of the most unexpected. In Tudor England, a *bully* was a good friend or beloved, and was used as a heart-felt form of address for people who were well-liked or admired, as in Shakespeare's *Henry V*:

The King's a bawcock [a good man], and a heart of gold …
I kiss his dirty shoe, and from heart-string
I love the lovely bully.

By a century later, *bully* had come to mean an overly aggressive, hectoring and intimidating ruffian – the only meaning that survives in modern English:

'Tis so ridiculous, but so true withal,
A bully cannot sleep without a brawl
— *The Third Satire of Juvenal* (1693), John Dryden

What prompted this change is unclear, but around Dryden's time *bully* was also being used of anyone who made a living protecting prostitutes on the streets of London, and so perhaps these protectors were the first 'bullies', who would have found themselves forced into confrontations with the women's would-be clients.]

Bully pulpit and *lunatic fringe* were both coined by Theodore Roosevelt.

◆

Teddy bears were named after Theodore Roosevelt.

[In November 1902, President Theodore 'Teddy' Roosevelt took part in a hunting trip in Mississippi. Although accounts of the trip vary, the President was apparently the only member of the party who failed to kill anything, and so as to not let him leave empty-handed, a young black bear was caught and chained to a tree for Roosevelt to shoot for sport. The President, however, refused and instead asked for the bear to be freed. Despite showing Roosevelt in a compassionate light, the incident was soon picked up on by satirists in the American press and a famous cartoon – depicting a bespectacled Roosevelt turning his back on a trembling bear cub, with the caption 'Drawing the line in Mississippi' – appeared in *The Washington Post* on 16 November 1902. The cartoon supposedly inspired the first real 'teddy bears', which began appearing in toy shops in New York just weeks later.]

◆

A group of polar bears is called an *aurora*.

◆

The Old English word for 'dawn', *dægrima*, literally means 'the rim of day'.

◆

A *rimbombo* is a loud, resonating noise or reverberation, like a rumble of thunder.

An *echo boom* is the follow-up to a *baby boom*.

> [Although today it's associated with the widespread increase in birth rate that followed the end of the Second World War in 1945, the earliest reference to a *baby boom* in fact comes from an 1880 newspaper article that described 'the Iowa baby boom' that followed the American Civil War: between 1860 and 1880, Iowa's population rose, staggeringly, by a million people. An *echo boom* typically ensues between twenty and forty years later, when those children born during a *baby boom* grow up and have children themselves – the UK's post-war baby boom in 1946 was followed by another increase in birth rate in 1964, and yet another in 1990.]

Echopraxia is the proper name for subconsciously mimicking someone else's movements or gestures – like yawning in response to a yawn.

A group of mockingbirds is called an *echo*.

The Aztec word for the mockingbird was *centzontlahtōleh*. It means 'possessor of 400 words'.

A *grad* is ¼₀₀ of a circle – or ¹⁄₁₀₀ of a right angle, or ⁹⁄₁₀ of a degree.

The expression *possession is nine-tenths of the law* was originally 'eleven-twelfths of the law'. No one knows why it changed.

◆

To gammon the twelve means 'to cheat a jury'.

◆

In American legal slang, to use the *Chewbacca defence* means to present a jury with an illogical or entirely unrelated argument in order to confuse them and distract from the real issue of the trial.

> [When the American football star O. J. Simpson was accused of the murder of his ex-wife in June 1994, part of the case for the prosecution rested on a bloodstained leather glove found in the driveway of his LA home. The glove, however, was shown by the defence team to be too small to fit Simpson's hand, and when the time came for closing arguments his lawyer, Johnnie Cochrane, famously told the jury, 'if it doesn't fit, you must acquit'. His glib attempt to boil down an eight-month murder trial to a question of whether or not a glove fitted a man's hand was successful (Simpson was acquitted in October 1995), but it was nevertheless seen by some commentators as an example of *ignoratio elenchi* – a guileful rhetorical technique in which a logical yet entirely unrelated argument is put forward simply to cloud the real issue at hand.
>
> In 1998, Cochrane's defence was satirised in an episode of the comedy series *South Park*, in which he was portrayed employing the 'Chewbacca defence' by pointing out to a jury that the *Star Wars* character Chewbacca lives on the planet Endor but is from the planet Kashyyyk – a fact, he repeatedly claims, which 'does not make sense'. Using the *Chewbacca defence* soon slipped into American legal and political slang, and has remained in occasional use ever since.]

♦

Jargogle, allemang, disparple and *mingle-mangle* all mean 'to throw into confusion', or 'mix up'.

♦

Hodge-podge, gallimaufry and *pot-pourri* were all originally the names of stews.

♦

The Greek playwright Aristophanes' comedy *The Assemblywomen*, written in 391 BC, contains the name of a stew called *lopadotemachoselachogaleokranioleipsanodrim hypotrimmatosilphioparaomelitokatakechymenokichlepikossy phophattoperisteralektryonoptekephalliokigklopeleiolagoiosir aiobaphetraganopterygon.*

> [This is just one English rendering of a 171-letter Greek word, λοπαδοτεμαχοσελαχογαλεοκρανιολειψανοδρι-μυποτριμματοσιλφιοκα ραβομελιτοκατακεχυμενοκιχλεπικοσσυφοφαττοπεριστεραλεκτρυονοπ τοκεφαλλιοκιγκλο-πελειολαγωοσιραιοβαφητραγανοπτερύγων, which is considered the longest word ever to have appeared in literature. It's comprised of at least twenty-seven different word roots, amongst them the names of all of the stew's main ingredients, including honey (*meli*), boiled wine (*siraion*), crayfish (*karabos*), dove (*peleia*), wood pigeon (*phatta*), thrush (*kikhle*), chicken (*alektruon*), hare (*lagoos*), slices of fish (*temakhos*), dogfish heads (*galeos kranion*), and roasted grebe brains (*optos kephalion kinklos*).]

♦

Shakespeare's longest word was *honorificabilitudinitatibus* in *Love's Labour's Lost*. It means 'honourability'.

[In Act V, scene i of *Love's Labour's Lost*, the stuffy schoolmaster Holofernes and his friend Nathaniel enjoy a long and absurd dialogue, partly in English and partly in Latin, in which they each try to appear as intelligent as possible while mocking the other characters' ignorance. They are soon joined by Costard, a clownish bumpkin who despite appearances proves no less witty and erudite:

> I marvel thy master hath not eaten thee for a word, for thou art not so long by the head as honorificabilitudinitatibus.

Surprisingly, *honorificabilitudinitatibus* is neither a Shakespearean invention nor a nonsense word but actually a derivative of the Latin word *honorificabilitudinitas*, meaning 'honourableness', which has been found in written texts dating back to the thirteenth century; an English equivalent, *honorificabilitudinity*, has been in, albeit infrequent, use since the mid-1600s. *Honorificabilitudinitatibus* is also, incidentally, the longest known word comprised entirely of alternating consonants and vowels.]

◆

The full name of *titin*, a protein that controls the contraction of muscles, has 189,819 letters.

◆

The longest palindrome in the *Oxford English Dictionary* is *tattarrattat*, coined by James Joyce to represent the sound of a knock on a door.

◆

Typewriter is one of the longest words that can be spelled using only the top row of keys on a qwerty keyboard.

[Appropriately enough, *typewrite*, *typewrote* and the ten-letter word *typewriter* can all be spelled using just the top row of a qwerty keyboard, alongside other ten-letter examples like *perpetuity*, *peppertree*, *repertoire* and *proprietor* – although if hyphens are allowed, the twelve-letter *teeter-totter*, another name for a seesaw, becomes the longest overall.

Thanks to its four vowels, the top row – QWERTYUIOP – is by far the most fruitful of the three on a qwerty keyboard, and its letters can be used to make more than 500 English words including *puppetry*, *etiquette*, *torturer*, *prototype*, *tripwire*, *pirouette* and *territory*. The single vowel found on the middle row – ASDFGHJKL – limits its total to roughly 200, including *flasks*, *skalds*, *salads*, *Alaska*, *alfalfa* and, longest of all, *haggadahs*, the name of certain Jewish scriptures. The bottom row – ZXCVBNM – contains no vowels, and can only be used to create onomatopoeic formations like *zzz* and *mmm*.]

♦

Increasing the size of a typeface by one *point* means increasing it by ½₂ of an inch.

[The precise size of a *point* – the smallest whole unit used in printing – has varied considerably since its origins in the days of metal printing presses, when it initially ranged from anywhere between 0.18–0.4mm. With the rise of desktop publishing in the 1980s and 90s however, the *point* was finally standardised to ½₂ of an inch, or 0.35mm. Twelve points, incidentally, make a *pica*.]

♦

Three-quarters of an inch is called a *finger*.

♦

A fingernail can also be called an *unguicule*.

♦

Telling someone's fortune by examining their fingernails is called *onychomancy*.

♦

Bibliomancy is a form of divination in which a book is allowed to fall open at random and a fortune is interpreted from the page at which it opens.

♦

Individual letters of the alphabet were once called *bookstaves*.

♦

The equivalent of the letter A in Egyptian hieroglyphics was a picture of an ox's head.

♦

If you were to write out every English number name in full (*one, two, three* ...) you wouldn't use a single letter B until you reached *one billion*.

> [You also wouldn't need a D until you reached *one hundred*; an M until you reached *one million*; and a C until you reached *one octillion* – or 1,000,000,000,000,000,000,000,000,000 (10^{27}). And no matter how high you counted, you would never need a J, K or Z.]

♦

In the American Army, laxatives were once called *CC pills* – an abbreviation of 'compound cathartic'.

♦

The D of *D-Day* doesn't stand for anything.

[The idea that the D of *D-Day* stands for 'departure' or 'disembarkation' – especially given its association with the Normandy Landings – is a myth. The fact is simply that while military operations are being planned, it's not always immediately clear when they will take place. As a result, their future start date, whenever that may be, is referred to as 'D-Day', and this acts as a placeholder until a final date can be set. If anything, the D could be said to *derive* from the word 'day' (indeed, the French equivalent is *J-Jour*) but it certainly doesn't stand for it.]

◆

Eleven per cent of the entire English language is just the letter E.

◆

The earliest recorded use of the F-word dates from 1475.

[*Fuck* is thought to be an ancient English taboo word that was presumably used in Anglo-Saxon England but never written down – or, at least, was never written in the kinds of documents that tended to survive from one generation to the next. Its earliest appearance in print is in an anonymous part-Latin poem entitled *Flen, flyys* ('Fleas, flies'), seemingly written in Cambridgeshire circa 1475:

> Fratres Carmeli navigant in a bothe apud Eli,
> Non sunt in cœli, quia gxddbov xxkxzt pg ifmk.
> [*Carmelite brothers sail in a boat around Ely,*
> *They aren't in heaven, because they fuck the wives of Ely*]

If it's hard to see where *fuck* appears in these original lines, then that's the whole point – the last four words of the second line here are in code, with each letter substituted for its alphabetical neighbour in an attempt to disguise its true content.

If part-Latin and part-encrypted poems are excluded, then the earliest real record of the F-word comes from the Scots poet William Dunbar's 'A Brash of Wowing' ('A Bout of Wooing') written in 1503:

> As with the glaikis he wer ovirgane.
> Yit be his feiris, he wald haue fukkit:
> 'Ye brek my hairt, my bony ane'.
> [*As with desire he was overcome.*
> *Yet be his behaviour, he would have fucked her:*
> *'You break my heart, my bonny one'.*]

This was followed only a few decades later by the first modern spelling of *fuck*, in the Scottish playwright Sir David Lindsay's *Satire of the Three Estates*, first performed in 1540:

> Bischops ar blist, howbeit that they be waryit,
> For thay may fuck thair fill, and be vnmaryit.
> [*Bishops are blessed, though they be cursed,*
> *For they may fuck their fill and stay unmarried.*]

Whether Lindsay's 'bischops' were also from Ely is unknown.]

♦

The G of *G-spot* stands for 'Gräfenberg', the surname of a German gynaecologist who first described 'an erogenous zone' in 1944.

♦

The letter H used to be called *aha*.

♦

The dot above a lower case *i* or *j* is called a *tittle*.

♦

K is the least frequently used letter of the alphabet in Spanish and Italian.

[K is only the sixth least-used letter in English (after Q, J, Z, X and V), but in Romance languages like Spanish and Italian – and French for that matter, in which only W is used any less frequently – K tends only to appear in foreign loan words, like the Spanish *kerosén* and Italian *karatè*. Languages like these are largely derived from Latin, which historically tended to alter the Greek *kappa*, K, to a Roman C when Greek-origin words first began to appear in Latin texts.]

◆

The three Ls of *frillless* make it the only unhyphenated word in the *Oxford English Dictionary* with three consecutive identical consonants.

[As a rule, the English language doesn't tend to allow three consecutive identical letters, outside of humorous and onomatopoeic inventions like *mmm*, *brrr* and *zzz*. On some rare occasions, though, a trio of identical letters can appear unavoidable and requires some kind of alteration or compromise to circumvent it: *seer* ('one who sees') and *freer* ('more free'), for instance, have been forced to lose a letter in order to avoid three consecutive Es (although some nineteenth-century editors preferred *seeër* and *freeër*). Likewise the old Scottish counties of *Ross-shire* and *Inverness-shire* were forced to hyphenate their names in order to avoid three consecutive Ss. The triple L of *frillless*, however, has been left intact in the *Oxford English Dictionary* despite a number of comparative words (like *wall-less*, *smell-less*, *skill-less*) being divided in two.]

◆

In the eighteenth century, *to carry an M under your girdle* meant 'to address someone as "mister" or "mistress"'.

The N of *PIN* stands for 'number'.

[*PIN* stands for 'personal identification number', so saying 'PIN number' really means saying 'personal identification number number'. Other unintentional repetitions can be found in *ATM machine* ('automated teller machine machine'), *ABS system* ('anti-lock braking system system'), *HIV virus* ('human immunodeficiency virus virus'), *AC current* ('alternating current current'), and *please RSVP* – an unwitting English/French mishmash of 'please respond please'. Needlessly repeating words like this that don't need repeating because its needless to do so is known as redundancy in linguistic terms, but when it happens to the words disguised inside an acronym it might, as *New Scientist* magazine explained in 2001, be better known as 'RAS syndrome' – or 'redundant acronym syndrome syndrome'.]

The O blood group should really be called 'zero'.

[The ABO blood group system was developed in the early 1900s by the Austrian scientist Karl Landsteiner, who was awarded the Nobel Prize for Medicine for his work in 1930. Landsteiner's research involved mixing together the bloods of a number of different people, from which he was able to recognise three basic blood types depending on how they reacted to one another: type A blood reacted badly to type B; B reacted badly to type A; and C showed no adverse reaction at all. Landsteiner theorised that the reactions between certain blood types was caused by antigens that attacked incompatible blood groups, and so as it was seemingly compatible with any blood group, Type C presumably lacked these antigens and became known as 'zero'. To ensure that all three main blood groups have alphabetical names, however, this 'zero' group is usually called 'O'.]

In the NATO phonetic alphabet, P stands for 'papa'. In the First World War Royal Navy alphabet, it stood for 'pudding'.

◆

In written English, only one letter in every 510 is a Q.

◆

The Czech word *ráčkovat* means 'to pronounce your Rs incorrectly'.

◆

The 'double-S' symbol used in German, ß, is called an *Eszett*.

◆

No one knows why things are *done to a T*.

[Everything from a golfer's tee to a draughtsman's T-square has been proposed as possible origins of *to a T*, which has been used in English since the seventeenth century to mean 'precisely' or 'exactly'. Its earliest record comes from an anonymous and snappily titled work of fiction called *Humours and Conversations of the Town, Expos'd in Two Dialogues, The First of the Men, The Second of the Women*, written in 1693:

As for your Country Attorney ... at the best Inn he takes up his standing, whilst all the under Villages and Towns-men come to him for Redress; which he does to a T.

The 'T' rather than 'tee' spelling here might point towards the T-square theory, but muddying things further is this line from *The Woman Hater* (1607), a Jacobean stage comedy by Francis Beaumont, which dates from almost a century earlier:

I'll quote him to a tittle: Let him speak wisely, and plainly, and as hidden as a' can, Or I shall crush him

A 'tittle', as we now know, is the dot or stroke above a lower case *i* or *j*, but it's being used figuratively here to mean 'a tiny amount': 'I'll quote him to a tittle' implies 'I'll watch his every move', or 'I'll observe even his slightest expressions'. *To a T* could ultimately be an abbreviation of *to a tittle*, implying something along the lines of 'every slightest detail has been done correctly' – like *dotting your Is and crossing your Ts*. As it stands, however, the true origins here remain a mystery.]

♦

The U of *U-boat* – or *Unterseeboot* in German – stands for 'undersea'.

♦

Using V for five in Roman numerals is thought to come from the practice of double-marking the fifth of a set of five tally marks.

♦

W is the only letter with a polysyllabic name, so there are three times as many syllables in *www* as there are in *world wide web*.

♦

The only word Shakespeare used that begins with an X was *Xanthippe*.

[Xanthippe was the wife of Socrates who was unflatteringly described in Xenophon's *Symposium*, a dialogue written circa 368 BC, as the 'the most difficult woman not just of this generation … but of all the generations past and yet to come'. Admittedly, other Greek writers were less insulting to Xanthippe (and in fact Xenophon himself later portrayed her as a kind and doting mother in his *Memorabilia*, circa 371 BC), but, as the saying goes, mud sticks: Xanthippe's reputation as a belligerent, difficult woman was ensured and survived long into the Middle Ages, with Shakespeare's Petruchio describing Katherine in *The Taming of the Shrew* as 'as curst and shrewd as Socrates' Xanthippe – or worse' (I.ii).]

♦

The letter Y was once called the 'Greek Y', or y *Graeca*.

♦

Samuel Morse presumed that Z was the least used letter of the alphabet. It's actually the third least used, after Q and J.

[When it came to assigning different combinations of dots and dashes to letters to create his code, Samuel Morse needed to know their frequencies, so that the shortest and easiest combinations could be assigned to the commonest letters, and *vice versa*. To do this, Morse (or rather his oft-overlooked collaborator, Alfred Vail) set about painstakingly counting the individual letters of metal type in a local printworks: they found there were 12,000 letter Es and 9,000 Ts, but only 500 Qs, 400 Js and Xs, and just 200 Zs. E and T were ultimately given the shortest possible codes, [·] and [-], while Q became [----], J [·---], X [-··-] and Z [--··]. Although letter frequency statistics are notoriously tricky subjects, according to the *Oxford English Dictionary*, Q is actually the least used letter of alphabet, followed by J, Z and X respectively.]

♦

The *ampersand*, &, was once considered the twenty-seventh letter of the alphabet.

[Up until the early 1900s the ampersand, &, was widely considered a letter of the alphabet and listed in final place after Z. At the time, it was also customary to preface letters of the alphabet that could be confused with single-letter words (like I and A) with the Latin phrase *per se*, 'by itself', and so as to avoid confusion between '&' and 'and', the alphabet typically ended 'X, Y, Z and *per se* &'. This final 'and per se and' eventually ran together, and sometime in the mid-1800s the name *ampersand* was born.]

♦

The question mark is thought by some to be derived from the Latin word for 'question', *quaestio*.

[A number of theories attempt to explain where the question mark comes from, of which this fairly convoluted Latin theory is just one. In the Middle Ages, the Latin *quaestio* was often abbreviated to *qo.*, which was used to mark sentences written in the interrogative (i.e. question-asking) mood. Over time, and to save much-needed space on each line of text, the *q* and *o* began to be written one atop the other and, so the theory goes, eventually combined to form '?'. As neat a theory as this is, the evidence to support it is lacking, and an alternative theory – that the question mark derived from a curled line or 'tilde' followed by a dot (~·) – seems more likely in comparison.]

♦

In the seventeenth century, a reverse question mark ⸮, called a *punctus percontativus*, was used to indicate that the preceding question was ironic or rhetorical.

[Given how potentially useful a symbol like this could be, especially in the age of the emoticon, it's both surprising and disappointing to find that it's never truly caught on, and even in its heyday the *punctus percontativus* – or 'percontative point' – was relatively rarely used. Conceived by the London printer Henry Denham in the 1580s, the problem from the outset was that few other printers besides Denham had the means to custom-make their own *percontativus* piece of type at the time (although some made do with an upside-down semicolon), and as a result it had all but disappeared from the language barely fifty years after its invention. Today, the only notable writer whose works made use of the symbol was the seventeenth-century poet Robert Herrick, best known for 'Gather ye rosebuds while ye may'.]

◆

A *rhetorical accent* is the repositioning of the accent or stress in a sentence in order to alter its meaning – like 'you said *that*?', 'you *said* that?', or, '*you* said that?'

◆

The earliest reference to someone well-spoken being described as having *a plum in their mouth* dates from 1553.

◆

A *plumcot* is a cross between a plum and an apricot.

◆

An *etaerio* is a fruit comprised of several smaller individual fruits or parts merged together, like a raspberry. It's also the most likely seven-letter word to be picked out of a bag of Scrabble tiles at the start of a game.

[There are one hundred lettered tiles in the bag at the start of a standard game of Scrabble, and given that some tiles are more numerous than others (there are twelve Es, nine As and Is, eight Os, and so on), a player picking seven tiles out at random will find themselves picking one of around 3,000,000 possible combinations. Not all of these combinations can be rearranged into valid seven-letter words of course, but you've approximately a one in 10,000 chance of picking the letters of *etaerio* on your first go, as well as one in 20,000 chance of picking *senator* or *retinas*, and a one in 30,000 chance of picking *realise*. Conversely, despite odds of one in 20,000,000, you'll no doubt find yourself sitting in front of a rack of seven Es at some point during the game.]

♦

A *hardscrabble* is a barren or inhospitable place where survival or making a living would be immensely difficult.

♦

The Arabic word for 'desert' is *sahara*. The Mongolian word for 'desert' is *gobi*. So 'Sahara Desert' and 'Gobi Desert' both mean 'desert desert'.

[So-called tautological place names are actually surprisingly common around the world, and typically come into existence when speakers of two different languages come into contact with each other. Other notable examples include the Mississippi River, which means 'big river river' in Algonquin and English; the La Brea Tar Pits, which are the 'tar tar pits' in Spanish and English; and East Timor, which takes its name from the Malay word for 'east', *timur*, and so literally means 'east east'. Perhaps the best example of all however is Torpenhow Hill in Cumbria – although the authenticity of the name is disputed, it nevertheless combines identical Old English (*tor*), Welsh (*penn*), Norse (*haugr*) and Modern English components, to come to mean 'hill hill hill hill'.]

♦

Alcove, cotton, ghoul, algebra, mascara, zero and *coffee* all derive from Arabic.

♦

A *kaffeeklatscher* is someone who gossips over a cup coffee.

◆

The insulating cardboard sleeve placed around a paper cup of coffee is called a *zarf*.

> [*Zarf* is the Arabic word for 'vessel', which was adopted into English via Egypt in the early nineteenth century. Strictly speaking, a *zarf* should actually be an ornamental metal holder – essentially a handle and saucer combined – that supports a hot cup without it burning your hand:
>
> > The coffee-cup … is small; generally not holding quite an ounce and a half of liquid. It is of porcelain … and being without a handle, is placed within another cup (called 'zarf') of silver or brass, according to the circumstances of the owner, and, both in shape and size, nearly resembling our egg-cup.
> > — *An Account of the Manners and Customers of The Modern Egyptians* (1836), Edward William Lane
>
> Since the early 2000s however, *zarf* has been commandeered by fast food chains and take-out coffee retailers to come to refer to a so-called 'coffee-clutch' or 'java-jacket' – the insulating cardboard sleeve placed around a disposable coffee cup.]

◆

To fly off the handle derives from lumberjacks' axe-heads coming loose during use.

◆

A female lumberjack is a *lumberjill*.

◆

In Victorian slang, a *lumber house* was a building where thieves would store their stolen property.

◆

A *kleptoparasite* is a creature that steals food from other animals.

◆

Parasite literally means 'eating beside'. In Ancient Greece, it referred to someone who ate at someone else's table.

◆

The Scots Gaelic word *sgiomlaireachd* means 'someone who only drops by at mealtimes'.

> [*Sgiomlaireachd* – which, despite appearances, is roughly pronounced 'skeum-lee-reekh' – is derived from the Gaelic word for 'beg' or 'intrude', *sgimilear*. It's essentially the Scots equivalent of 'mooching' or 'scrounging', or 'the low arts of a parasite' as one nineteenth-century *Dictionary of the Gaelic Language* (1831) defined it. Or else:
>
>> [The] mean habits of popping in upon people at meals; living and doing nothing about gentlemen's kitchens.
>> — *The Argyllshire Pronouncing Gaelic Dictionary* (1832),
>> Neil MacAlpine]

◆

The Inuit word *iktsuarpok* means 'the feeling of anticipation that a visitor is about to arrive, which compels you to repeatedly look outside'.

◆

Angel visits are catch-ups with friends that are all too rare and few and far between.

◆

The rhetorical expression *how many angels can dance on the head of a pin?* has been used since the seventeenth century to refer to an utterly pointless and time-wasting debate or area of research.

[If the question *how many angels can dance on the head of a pin?* sounds ludicrous, then that's the whole point. Much to the annoyance of later philosophers from the Middle Ages onwards, mediaeval thinkers like Thomas Aquinas and John Duns Scotus (whose followers, incidentally, were the first 'dunces') spent much of their time contemplating bizarre queries precisely like this: Aquinas' *Summa Theologica*, a vast theological textbook written in the nine years leading up to his death in 1274, includes whole chapters discussing issues like 'whether an angel is composed of matter and form?', 'whether an angel can be in several places at once?', and 'whether the angels differ in species?'. At no point, however, does he discuss 'how many angels can dance on the head of a pin', which, it seems, is a much later invention concocted by philosophers in the Middle Ages looking to ridicule Aquinas and his contemporaries for their fondness for discussing what they saw as utterly pointless issues. Writing in 1638, the English theologian William Chillingworth was apparently the first person to accuse 'the divines of England' of 'prevaricating in the religion which they profess', and wasting their time by debating 'whether a million of angels may not sit upon a needle's point'. His words were soon taken up by other equally contemptuous writers, and over time came to refer simply to any pointless or impractical investigation.

But how many angels can dance on the head of a pin? According to 'Quantum Gravity Treatment of the Angel Density Problem' (2001), an article by Dr Andres Sandberg of Stockholm's Royal Institute of Technology, a total of 8.6766×10^{49}.]

◆

A *mateotechny* is an utterly pointless scientific study.

◆

An *apagoge* is a demonstration that doesn't prove anything, but only makes its alternative look absurd.

◆

Preposterous derives from the Latin words for 'before' and 'after'.

[*Preposterous* takes its absurd meaning from the fact that it combines two contradictory words – *prae*, the Latin word for 'before', and *posterus*, meaning 'after' or 'subsequent'. In fact, when it first appeared in the language in the early 1500s, it literally meant 'inverted', or 'having what should come last first'.

Preposterous is one of a handful of so-called oxymoronic words comprised of two opposing word roots, alongside *pianoforte* (literally 'soft-loud'), *sophomore* (derived from the Greek words for 'wisdom' and 'fool'), *firewater* (a nineteenth-century nickname for particularly powerful alcohol), and *bridegroom* (which literally means 'bride-man'). Perhaps best of all, however, is the criminally underused word *chantepleure*, a fourteenth-century French term used by Geoffrey Chaucer, which describes a mixture of alternating or simultaneous happiness and sadness; it literally means 'singing and crying'.]

◆

The French phrase *après moi le deluge* – 'after me the flood' – is used to imply a total indifference to what might happen after you have gone.

♦

In the sixteenth century *suds* were floodwaters, or the mud and grime left behind by a flood as it recedes.

♦

Cataclysms and *debacles* were both originally floods.

> [*Cataclysm* is derived via French and Latin from the Ancient Greek word *kataklysmos*, which literally meant 'washed down', but more often than not was used to imply being washed away by floodwater. On its earliest appearance in English in the early 1600s, it often referred specifically to the flood that swept all but Noah's Ark from the face of the Earth in the Old Testament, with the Elizabethan writer Thomas Heywood making reference to the 'first Universall Cataclisme' in 1637. *Debacle* meanwhile is derived from the French verb *débâcler*, meaning 'to unleash' or 'set free', and originally referred to the breaking up of ice and thawing of snow in spring. The French equivalent of a financial or stock market crash, incidentally, is a *débâcle financière*.]

♦

A *disaster* is literally an 'ill-starred' catastrophe, caused by an astrological misalignment.

> [The *–aster* of *disaster* is the same as in *asteroid* and *asterisk*, and can ultimately be traced back to the Latin and Greek words for 'star'. The implication is clearly that ill-fated or disastrous events here on earth can be blamed on misalignments or displacements of the stars and planets – or, as one *Derivative Dictionary of the English Language* (1783)

put it, 'an event happening (according to the absurd system of astrology) under the malignant influence of an unlucky planet'.

> This is the excellent foppery of the world, that when we are sick in fortune – often the surfeit of our own behaviour – we make guilty of our disasters the sun, the moon, and the stars; as if we were villains by necessity, fools by heavenly compulsion.
>
> — *King Lear* (I.ii), William Shakespeare]

◆

A starfish's arm is called a *radius*.

◆

***Exocet* missiles take their name from the French word for flying fish.**

◆

***Torpedo* is the Latin word for the stingray.**

◆

***Stingo* is a Tudor name for strong ale. *To give someone hot stingo* meant to punish or reprimand them.**

◆

A *choaking-pye* was an eighteenth-century punishment or practical joke in which smoke was blown up a victim's nose while they slept.

> [In his *Dictionary of the Vulgar Tongue* (1785), the lexicographer Francis Grose defined a *choaking-pye* as:
>
> > A punishment inflicted on any person sleeping in company: it

consists in wrapping up cotton in a case or tube of paper, setting
it on fire, and directing the smoke up the nostrils of the sleeper.]

♦

An *askefise* – literally an 'ash-blower' – is a cowardly man
who avoids military service to stay at home and help
tend the fire.

♦

Focus was the Roman word for a fireplace, the 'focal
point' of a household.

♦

The process of making something fireproof is called
dephlogistication.

♦

The power to control fire is called *ignipotence*.

♦

The Finnish for 'gather the whole bonfire together' is
kokoo kokoon koko kokko.

♦

Bonfires were originally 'bone-fires' in which bones
would be ceremonially burnt, or on which martyrs and
heretics would be burnt to death.

♦

In Old English, *November* was known as *Blotmonað*, meaning 'blood-month'.

> [The name *Blotmonað* apparently refers to the time of year when the Anglo-Saxons would have slaughtered and butchered their livestock ahead of the winter, ensuring that they had a store of food ready for the harshest season of the year.]

♦

An *Aceldama* is a place of great bloodshed or slaughter named after the field outside Jerusalem that Judas purchased with the silver he was paid to betray Jesus.

♦

The 'Jerusalem' of *Jerusalem artichoke* is a corruption of the Italian word for 'sunflower', *girasole*.

♦

In French, someone who falls in love with everyone they meet is said 'to have a heart like an artichoke', *avoir un cœur d'artichaut*.

♦

In some Scots dialects, artichokes are called *worry-baldies*.

♦

Phalacrophobia is the fear of becoming bald.

♦

Cormorants were once known as *phalacrocoraces*, or 'bald ravens'.

◆

A group of cormorants is called a *gulp*.

◆

Slonk, *yaffle*, *gamf*, *frample* and *gollop* all mean 'to swallow noisily', or 'to eat greedily'.

◆

A *hirondelle de nuit*, or 'night-swallow', is an old French nickname for a prostitute.

◆

In Shakespearean English, a *customer* was a prostitute.

> [*Customer* has always been used to mean 'purchaser' or 'buyer' ever since it first began to appear in English in the fifteenth century, but originally it could also be used of anyone involved in a transaction or trade, a sense that the ever-inventive Shakespeare took one step further in *Othello* (IV.i):
>
> > I marry her! What! A customer! Prithee bear some charity to my wit: do not think it so unwholesome.
>
> The use of *customer* to mean 'prostitute' was short-lived, and unlike many of Shakespeare's more inventive coinages seemingly failed to catch on – Samuel Johnson stated that it was 'now obsolete' in his dictionary, and the *Oxford English Dictionary* lists only one other instance of it, in Shakespeare's *All's Well That Ends Well*.]

◆

A *lagniappe* is a free gift or gratuity given to a customer alongside their purchase.

♦

A *flumpence* is an insultingly small tip or payment.

♦

In nineteenth-century England, a *penny hang* was a basement room with a series of ropes strung across it. Anyone without anywhere to stay for the night could pay to spend the night sleeping against the ropes.

♦

A kink or knot in a piece of rope is called a *chinkle*.

♦

The central thread of a rope, the sole of a horse's foot, and the innermost part of a tree trunk are all known as the *heart*.

♦

Angina is the Polish word for tonsillitis.

♦

Softheartedness is an anagram of 'sheds tears often'.

♦

A *crying room* is a soundproof room, first introduced in American cinemas in the 1930s for women with babies and children.

To cry roast meat was a Tudor expression meaning 'to brag', or 'to boast about your own successes'.

◆

In Victorian English, telling someone not *to chant the poker* meant telling them not to exaggerate a story.

◆

A *croupier* was originally someone who sat behind a rider on the hindquarters of a horse, that is, one who rode behind the 'croup'.

◆

A *gormagon* is 'a monster with six eyes, three mouths, four arms, eight legs, five on one side and three on the other, three arses, two tarses [penises], and a c—t upon its back'.

> [*Gormagon* is apparently a blend of 'gorgon' and 'dragon', although the 'monster' being crudely (yet entirely accurately) described here sounds unlike either of them. In fact, this definition is taken from Francis Grose's appropriately titled *Dictionary of the Vulgar Tongue* (1785), and is actually a longstanding and somewhat cryptic joke referring, as Grose later clarified, to 'a man on horseback, with a woman behind him'.]

◆

Cryptozoology is the study of monsters and creatures not proven to exist.

◆

Yeti is thought to derive from a Tibetan word, *yeh-teh*, meaning 'little manlike animal'.

◆

A *middelmannetjie* – a 'little man in the middle' in Afrikaans – is the raised ridge of earth formed between two sunken tyre tracks.

◆

To track up the dancers meant 'to go upstairs' in old criminal slang.

◆

In the eighteenth century, a *figure dancer* was a criminal or forger who specialised in altering the numbers on banknotes.

◆

The proper name for a cancan dancer is *cancaneuse*.

◆

The French verb *cancaner* means both 'to gossip', and 'to quack like a duck'.

◆

The *duck's ass* was a gents' hairstyle popular in America in the 1950s.

> [Also called a *ducktail* or a *DA*, the *duck's ass* hairstyle apparently surfaced in Philadelphia in the early 1940s, before quickly gaining

popularity elsewhere. It involved slicking the hair on the back of the head forwards, holding it in place with pomade, with a clear centre parting down from the crown of the head to the back of the neck, so that it apparently resembled the rear end of a duck. The rest of the hair was either left untidy or, more usually, styled up and back, and gelled in place on top of the head.]

♦

Buttock-mail was a tax once levied on people in Scotland who had sex out of wedlock.

[Brought in as one of the Poor Law Taxes introduced in Scotland from the mid-1500s onwards, *buttock-mail* was really more of a fine that could be imposed by an ecclesiastical court on anyone caught with a prostitute (a *buttock* in seventeenth-century slang), or who had been caught having sex outside of marriage. At the time, Scotland's strict Presbyterian courts were responsible for ensuring the moral behaviour of the people, and this tax, introduced under James VI in 1595, was their attempt to enforce chastity while simultaneously punishing adulterers and fornicators. Anyone literally caught *in flagrante delicto* would ordinarily be punished by being made to sit on a 'Stool of Repentance' in their local church, but the payment of *buttock-mail* commuted this sentence and allowed the offender in question to avoid public humiliation and to remain anonymous:

What! D'ye think the lads wi' the kilts will care for yer synods and yer presbyteries, and yer buttock-mail, and yer stool o' repentance? Vengeance on the black face o't! Mony an honester woman's been set upon it than streeks doon [i.e. lies down] beside ony Whig in the country.

— *Waverley* (1814), Sir Walter Scott]

♦

Pimpompet and *bumdockdousse* were seventeenth-century games whose only aim was apparently to kick other players in the backside.

♦

Kickie-wickie is a Shakespearean word for 'wife'.

♦

A *drachenfutter* is a gift given by a husband to placate his wife. It literally means 'dragon-feed' in German.

♦

Flapdragon is an old English parlour game in which players have to snatch raisins out of a pool of burning brandy.

[*Flapdragon* presumably dates back to Tudor England, if not earlier, and was traditionally played on Christmas Eve. Its earliest known references are all from Shakespeare, although unsurprisingly he chose to rework its meaning to refer figuratively to anything small or of little value ('Thou art easier swallowed than a flap-dragon', *Love's Labour's Lost* V.i), or to a sudden swallowing or engulfing ('But to make an end of the ship: to see how the sea flap-dragon'd it', *The Winter's Tale* III. iii). Flapdragon remained popular right through to the Victorian era, by which time the word had morphed into 'snapdragon' and gained an accompanying chant, 'The Song of the Snapdragon', recorded in *The Chambers Book of Days* (1893):

Here he comes with flaming bowl,
Don't he mean to take his toll,
Snip! Snap! Dragon!
Take care you don't take too much,
Be not greedy in your clutch,
Snip! Snap! Dragon!]

The Mandarin word for 'dinosaur', *kǒnglóng*, means 'fearsome dragon'.

◆

Velociraptor, *plagiarist*, *furuncle* and *ferret* all mean 'thief'.

◆

A group of ferrets is called a *fesnyng*.

> [Actually, a group of ferrets is called a *business* and has been since the mid-1400s, but sometime in its history the fifteenth-century word *besynes* was misread as *fesynes*, and then this too was misread and became *fesnyng*, which has since established itself as another perfectly acceptable group term – despite being derived from a misreading of a mistake – listed in a number of major dictionaries.]

◆

The *ichneumon* is an African mongoose that was once believed to crawl into crocodile's mouths and eat them from the inside out.

> [*Ichneumon* literally means 'hunter' or 'tracker' in Greek, and it seems the hunter's reputation for bravery in tackling potentially dangerous wild animals is the root of all later uses of the word. Aristotle first gave the name to a kind of wasp that he had observed actively hunting spiders. This led to it being attached to the Egyptian mongoose, which had long been held in high regard for its audacity in raiding the nests of crocodiles to get to the eggs inside. The mongoose's apparent habit of eating crocodiles from the inside is a myth presumably born out of its reputation for bravery, but in the eighteenth century it nevertheless inspired the Swedish naturalist Carl Linnaeus to name a family of

parasitic wasps after it: found throughout the tropics, *Ichneumonidae* lay their eggs in or on an unsuspecting host, who is then devoured from the inside out by the larvae when they hatch.]

◆

Named after an ancient logical puzzle, *crocodility* is specious reasoning, or an overly pedantic and fault-finding way of thinking.

[The 'Crocodile Dilemma' is a logical puzzle in the form of a fable, which apparently originated in Ancient Greece. Although numerous wordings and versions of it exist, the following account and its explanation, from an eighteenth-century textbook called *The Preceptor* (which, according to its full title, set out 'the first principles of polite learning … in a way most suitable for trying the Genius'), is perhaps the most thorough:

> A poor Woman begging a Crocodile, that had caught her Son walking by the River Side, to spare and restore him; was answered, That he would spare and restore him, provided she would give a true Answer to the Question he should propose: The Question was, *Will I restore thy son or not?* To this the poor Woman, suspecting a deceit, sorrowfully answered, *Thou wilt not*: And demanded to have him restored, because she had answered truly. Thou lyest, said the Crocodile, for if I restore him, thou hast not answered truly: I cannot therefore restore him without making thy Answer false.

The crocodile's paradox – i.e. if the woman answers correctly, he cannot do what he has agreed to without invalidating her answer – and his nit-picking way of working the problem out is the inspiration behind *crocodility*, which first appeared in the Irish lexicographer James Knowles' *Explanatory Dictionary of the English Language* (1835). Knowles defined *crocodility* as 'in logic, a captious, sophistical kind of argumentation', which is almost as perplexing a string of words as the problem itself.]

◆

The earliest record of the word *alligator* dates from 1542 as another word for someone who ties or 'alligates' things together.

◆

Merinthophobia is a fear of being tied up.

◆

Faleste was an old French capital punishment in which a victim would be tied up and left on a beach to be carried away by the tide.

◆

A *republican marriage* was a form of capital punishment used during the French Revolution in which a man and woman would be tied together and thrown into a river to drown.

◆

Inspired by a series of murders that took place during the French Revolution, to *septembrise* means 'to assassinate someone while they are in prison'.

[*Septembrising* is derived from the September Massacres, a series of bloody attacks on prisons that took place across Paris in 1792. The attacks were carried out by bands of hundreds of armed rebels, who had grown wary of the number of political and counter-revolutionary prisoners being held in the city's jail. For four days, 2–6 September, they launched a series of shockingly violent raids on prisons all across

Paris, which saw some 1,200 prisoners subjected to mob courts before being tortured, murdered and often horrifically mutilated – many were women and children, and more than 200 of those killed were priests who had simply refused to accept the Revolution's reorganisation of the church.]

♦

Pont Neuf means 'new bridge'. It is actually the oldest bridge in Paris.

♦

Anything *transpontine* is located on the opposite side of a bridge.

♦

Anything *interlacustrine* is located between two lakes.

♦

A *lacuna*, literally 'a small lake', is the 'gap' found when a word is translated from one language into another in which it has no obvious equivalent.

♦

The Congolese word *ilunga* is apparently the hardest known word to translate. It essentially means 'a person who is willing to forgive once, and perhaps twice, but never a third time'.

['Words', according to Samuel Johnson, 'are but the signs of ideas'. But sometimes those ideas are so complex that attempting to explain their full intricacies and implications in a definition is all but impossible.

Ilunga, a word taken from the Tshiluba language of the Democratic Republic of the Congo, is an example of precisely that, and in a survey of a thousand linguists and translators in 2004 was named the hardest known word to translate into English. The definition given above – as well as others in dictionaries and articles attempting to define the word in English terms – admittedly comes nowhere close to truly encapsulating *ilunga*'s full and complex meaning. All told, the tragedy is that if you don't already speak Tshiluba then you're unlikely ever to be able to fully understand and appreciate how wonderfully complex it is.]

♦

A *translation* was originally the removal and transferral of the remains of a saint from one place to another.

♦

A *saint* is a useless leftover piece of timber, so-called because it is only worth being sacrificed to the fire.

♦

Dice were once known as *St Hugh's bones*.

[Dice have been known as 'bones' since the fourteenth century, with even Geoffrey Chaucer making reference to some 'bicched bones' (probably meaning 'cursed' or 'notched') in his *Canterbury Tales*. St Hugh, meanwhile, is the patron saint of shoemakers, and the first item ever nicknamed 'St Hugh's bones' was actually a shoemaker's toolkit, probably in reference to the sound of the loose tools clanking like bones inside. By the early nineteenth century this nickname had come to also be applied to dice, in the similar sense of them rattling around in a player's hands.]

♦

San Pantaleone, a patron saint of Venice, is the origin of the word *pantaloons*.

♦

Venezuela means 'little Venice'.

♦

The phrase *play on words* was coined by Shakespeare in *The Merchant of Venice*.

♦

Pundigrion, *calembour*, *clench* and *quiblet* are all alternative names for puns.

♦

A *quibibble* is a pointless, trivial argument.

♦

Anything *quisquilious* is composed entirely of rubbish.

♦

A *quodlibetarian* is someone who talks endlessly of minor things, or who is happy to talk at length about any subject whatsoever.

♦

The Scots word *clishmaclaver* means 'idle, meaningless chatter'.

♦

Yill, an old Scots word for ale, means 'to entertain someone with beer', or 'to supply your lover with drink while wooing them'.

◆

Sphallolalia is flirtatious chatter that goes nowhere.

◆

The seventeenth-century word *firkytoodle* means 'to caress lovingly'.

◆

John Milton invented the word *lovelorn*.

◆

The Russian word *razbliuto* describes the sentimental feeling you have about someone you once loved but no longer do.

◆

The word *pamphlet* is derived from an anonymous mediaeval love poem called *Pamphilus, seu de Amore*.

[Very little is known of the origin of the Latin dramatic poem *Pamphilus, seu de Amore* ('Pamphilus, or About Love') other than that it was written somewhere on the continent (most likely France) in the late 1100s. What is known, however, is that it proved immensely popular: throughout the thirteenth century, its 720 lines were read, reread, reprinted and widely distributed across Europe, and references to it appear in the contemporary literature of everywhere from Norway in the north to Castile in the south. Students at the University of Paris were even reprimanded for disregarding more worthwhile material in favour of reading about the erotic adventures of the Greek hero Pamphilus and his lover Galatea.

It's the poem's popularity that is the origin of the modern *pamphlet* – *Pamphilus* became *Pamphilet* in French, a diminutive name partly based on the fact the poem wasn't quite long enough to be classed as a full book. Soon, this was being attached to any unbound document that didn't quite constitute a book, with the earliest independent reference to a 'little pamphilet' dating from the early 1400s.]

♦

Brochure is the French word for 'stitched'. It originally referred to a short booklet whose pages had been stitched not glued together.

♦

The medical name for pins-and-needles is *paraesthesia*.

♦

Iatrapistia is a lack of faith in doctors or medicine.

♦

The opposite of the *placebo* effect is the *nocebo* effect, wherein a patient reports feeling worse despite being given a harmless treatment.

♦

An *antephialtic* is a medicine or sleeping draught taken to protect against nightmares.

♦

Oneirocriticism is the interpretation of dreams.

◆

Talking in your sleep is called *somniloquency*.

◆

Conversation is an anagram of 'voices rant on'.

◆

Sialoquency is spraying saliva while talking.

◆

Fasting-spittle is saliva produced first thing in the morning before breakfast. It was once believed to have healing properties.

[The healing power of saliva is a particularly ancient superstition, mentioned as a cure for bloodshot eyes by the Roman scholar Pliny the Elder as far back as the first century AD, and even the Gospel of Mark (7:32–5) records Jesus using his spittle to cure a man's deafness. This curative practice lasted long into the Middle Ages, when the Tudor writer Thomas Lupton explained in his brilliantly titled *Thousand Notable Things on Various Subjects* (1579) that:

> The Fasting Spittle of a whole and sound person doth quite take away all Scurviness, Sawsflame, or Redness of the Face, Ringworms, Tetters, and all kinds of Pustules or Wheals by smearing or rubbing the infected place therewith.

An eighteenth-century London physician named Nicholas Robinson referred to fasting-spittle as 'the noble balsam of Nature' in his equally brilliantly titled *Treatise on the Virtues and Efficacy of a Crust of Bread* (1756), and, amongst a number of different treatments, advocated the use of a poultice made from chewed bread as 'an infallible cure' for corns, warts and gout. Robinson's treatise remained hugely popular long into the nineteenth century, running to several editions and even being published in America as recently as 1844.]

♦

A *jejunator* is someone who fasts.

♦

Jejunojejunostomy – a medical procedure in which the second part of the small intestine is bypassed – is the only word in the English language containing four letter Js.

[Excluding proper nouns and impossibly lengthy chemical names, no English word apparently contains more than nine appearances of the same letter: there are nine Is in *floccinaucinihilipilification*, 'the act of considering something worthless'; nine Ss in *possessionlessnesses*; and nine Us in *humuhumunukunukuapuaa*, the name of a species of Hawaiian triggerfish. Coming in a close second, there are eight Es in *peekeeneenee*, an alternative form of *piccaninny*, meaning 'very small'; and eight Os in *toomatoogooroo*, a New Zealand shrub. What makes *jejunojejunostomy* so remarkable, however, is the J is such an infrequent letter to begin with, and for the same reason the four Ks of *kakkak*, a type of Pacific Ocean bittern, are equally unusual, as are the three Qs in *quinquinquagintillion*, or 10^{168}; the four Vs of *oviovoviviparous*, describing internal-brooding fish that keep fertilised eggs inside their bodies before laying them; the three Xs of *hexahexaflexagon*, a six-edged, double-sided folding game; and the six Zs of *zenzizenzizenzic*.]

♦

The letter J was originally only a variation of the last I in a row of Roman numerals – so thirteen might be written XIIJ.

If every possible Roman numeral were listed alphabetically, the last number would always be thirty-eight – XXXVIII.

♦

The longest English word made entirely of Roman numerals is *cimicic*, a type of foul-smelling acid secreted by stinkbugs.

> [Although various versions and permutations of Roman numerals are recorded throughout history, the seven basic characters are I (1), V (5), X (10), L (50), C (100), D (500) and M (1,000). The fact that only one vowel is used, as well as two of the rarest letters in the English language, X and V, makes forming words from Roman numerals a somewhat restricted business, but the seven-letter *cimicic* is nevertheless closely followed by *imidic*, the name of another type of acid, as well as several more familiar five-letter words like *civic*, *mimic*, *civil*, *livid* and *vivid*.]

♦

The chemical element *bromine* is named after the Greek word for 'stink'.

♦

The chemical elements *yttrium*, *erbium*, *terbium* and *ytterbium* are all named after the Swedish village of Ytterby.

> [The tiny village of Ytterby on the outskirts of Stockholm is the site of a mine where, in the late 1700s, a rare earth mineral was discovered

and named *yttria*. Over the next eighty years, yttria was found to contain four new chemical elements, each of which was similarly given a name honouring its place of discovery: *yttrium* (atomic number 39) and *erbium* (68) are both used in lasers and LEDs; *terbium* (65) is used in sonar systems and fuel cells; and *ytterbium* (70), which is used to make the most accurate atomic clocks in the world.]

◆

Swedish wasn't the official language of Sweden until 2009.

[As many as nine out of ten Swedish people profess to being able to speak English, a fact that in recent years had led to calls for English to be recognised as a second rather than foreign language in the country. Understandably, these plans proved hugely controversial and in 2009, in an effort to reinforce the status of the native language above all others, the government made Swedish the official language of Sweden for the first time in the country's history.]

◆

The Swedish word for 'jealous', *svartsjuk*, means 'black-sick'.

◆

Easter Monday was known as 'Black Monday' in mediaeval England.

[The nickname 'Black Monday' apparently alludes to the fact that Easter Monday has long been considered a traditionally unlucky day – although no one is quite certain why. One theory refers to a bloody attack by group of Gaelic warriors on 500 English settlers in Dublin, which took place on Easter Monday, 6 April 1209. Another equally plausible explanation, outlined in the *Chronicles of London* in the fifteenth century, refers to an event of Easter Monday, 14 April 1360 when:

> Kyng Edward with his Oost lay byfore the Citee off Parys; the which was a ffoule Derke day … so bytter colde that syttyng on horse bak men dyed; Wherefore, vnto this day yt ys called blak Monday.
>
> [*Edward III with his company lay before the city of Paris; it was a foul, dark day … so bitter cold that, sitting on horseback, men died. Therefore, unto this day, it is called Black Monday.*]]

♦

The capital city of Tajikistan, Dushanbe, means 'Monday' in Tajik.

> [Dushanbe has been the official capital of the republic of Tajikistan since 1925, when it was little more than a town of around 6,000 people; it is now home to more than 750,000. Its name refers to the fact that the town grew out of a village whose local market was held on a Monday. In fact, *du shanbe* literally means 'two days after Saturday' in Tajik.]

♦

Monday is the only day of the week with a one-word anagram – 'dynamo'.

♦

A *hebdomadiversary* is a one-week anniversary.

♦

The German word for 'honeymoon', *Flitterwochen*, means 'tinsel-week'.

> [*Flitter* is an old-fashioned German word which, as well as

meaning 'tinsel' or 'sequins', is sometimes used more generally to mean 'trumpery' or 'frippery', gaudy and flashy articles of little real value. In the case of *Flitterwochen*, it presumably referred to the beads and ribbons that once used to decorate brides' veils.]

♦

A *gandermoon* is the month after a woman has given birth. A *gandermooner* is a husband who flirts with other women while his wife recovers from childbirth.

♦

A *sooterkin* is a monstrous mouse-like creature supposedly borne by women who sit on stovetops during pregnancy.

[In the Middle Ages, pregnant Dutch women apparently had a habit of sitting on stovetops to keep themselves warm. From this innocent practice came the myth of the *sooterkin*, a creature the Scottish physician John Maubray colourfully described in his midwifery textbook, *The Female Physician* (1724), as:

[…] a Monstrous little Animal, the likeness of any thing in shape and size to a MOODIWARP [a mole], having a hooked snout, fiery sparkling Eyes, a long round Neck and acuminated short Tail, of an extraordinary Agility of Feet. At first sight of the World's Light, it commonly Yells and Shrieks fearfully; and seeking for a Hole runs up and down like a little Demon, which indeed I took it for, the first time I saw it.

At the time, Maubray was one of Britain's leading obstetric physicians and his work revolutionised midwifery and made both hospitals and childbirth considerably safer for women. He was, however, a product of his time, and for all of his forward-thinking he was still firmly rooted in the folklore and superstition of the past: as well as writing the description above, Maubray even claimed to have helped deliver a sooterkin (or a 'sucker', as he called it) after a woman passenger on a ferry he was travelling on in Holland went into labour en route. What's more, two years after the publication of his *Female Physician*, he became embroiled in the trial of Mary Toft, a woman from Surrey who claimed to have given birth to a litter of rabbits – a claim Dr Maubray lent his full support to.

So why would one of Britain's foremost physicians believe such patently ludicrous ideas? Well, in the days long before heredity science, physicians like Maubray were left with little recourse but to believe in so-called 'maternal impression', a theory that claimed that everything a woman sees, feels or experiences during pregnancy could have a profound physical effect on her child. As Maubray explained:

> Whence is it then that we have so many deform'd Persons, crooked Bodies, ugly Aspects, distorted Mouths, wry Noses, and the like, in all Countries; but from the IMAGINATION of the Mother … Wherefore it is very wrong, and highly imprudent in Women that have conceived, to please themselves so much in playing with Dogs, Squirrels, Apes, &c. carrying them in their Laps or Bosoms, and feeding, kissing, or hugging them.

Precisely when it *is* prudent to carry a squirrel in your bosom, Maubrey failed to say.]

♦

The Inuit word *tukirummiaq* means 'any solid object that can be used to keep the feet of a woman in labour in place'.

♦

The *mid* of 'midwife' is a Middle English word meaning 'with'.

♦

Drawing rooms were originally called *withdrawing rooms*.

♦

A *withdrawal* was originally called a *withdraught*.

♦

Draughts was originally called *jeu de dames*. It literally means 'a game of ladies'.

♦

Jeu de paume was a precursor to tennis that was played without racquets. It literally means 'palm game'.

♦

Napalm is a contraction of *naphthenic* and *palmitic*, the names of two acids used in its manufacture.

♦

Aspirin was originally a trademark for acetylsalicylic acid.

[In the late nineteenth century, the German pharmaceutical company Bayer began selling synthesised acetylsalicylic acid under the trade name *Aspirin*. They marketed their discovery (which was actually based on the aborted research of the earlier French chemist, Charles Frédéric Gerhardt) as a less astringent and more easily digestible alternative to pure salicylic acid, various forms and preparations of which have been used to relieve pain since antiquity – even Hippocrates used powdered salicylate-rich willow bark to treat headaches and fevers in Ancient Greece. Aspirin proved an immensely profitable success for

Bayer, which led to fierce competition amongst rival pharmaceutical corporations to either imitate or better their product – all of which took place in the lead-up to the First World War.

With Europe torn apart and Germany thrown into disarray, the Treaty of Versailles, signed on 28 June 1919, set out a series of concessions that Germany was compelled to agree to following its surrender the previous year. Amongst all of the financial reparations and redrawn borders, the Treaty sought to remove Bayer's trademark of the name *Aspirin*, a clear sign of just how important and widespread its use had become. To this day, *aspirin* remains a free-to-use generic name in all of the Treaty's signatory nations, including the UK, America, France and Russia, while Bayer's trademark – *Aspirin* with a capital A – remains in place in all other world territories.]

◆

The trade name *Spandex* was coined as an anagram of 'expands'.

◆

A *blanagram* is a word that is an anagram of another, except for the substitution of one letter – like 'promiSe' and 'improVe'.

[The name *blanagram* comes from the world of competitive Scrabble playing, and denotes an anagram that takes into consideration a 'blank' tile – namely one that can be used to represent any letter of the alphabet. Depending on what dictionary is being consulted, some sets of Scrabble tiles have dozens of possible seven-letter blanagrams, including ENORST_ (which has thirty-one), AENRST_ (which has fifty-seven), and AEIRST_ (which can be rearranged to form as many as seventy possible words).]

◆

The German word *Verschlimmbesserung* means 'an intended improvement that actually ends up making something worse'.

♦

Meliorism is the general belief that things get better with time.

♦

The practice of trying to improve your memory is called *mnemotechny*.

♦

Oblivious should really mean 'having no memory of', not 'unaware'.

♦

The opposite of *déjà-vu* is *jamais-vu* – the unusual feeling that a familiar experience is actually something entirely new.

> [While *déjà-vu* means 'already seen' in French, *jamais-vu* literally means 'never seen' and, unlike *déjà-vu*, tends to affect a person's recognition of words and faces, rather than actions and situations. It is a genuine psychological phenomenon (and in extreme cases can be associated with forms of amnesia, schizophrenia and even epilepsy) but in less serious contexts is common in stressful or emotionally heightened everyday situations, accounting for students momentarily going blank in exams, or actors and musicians forgetting their lines or music partway through a performance. A notable example of *jamais-vu* is a trait known as 'semantic satiation', wherein a person uses a word or phrase so many times that it begins to lose all meaning. An experiment in 2006

saw two-thirds of people experiencing symptoms of *jamais-vu* when asked to write out the word 'door' thirty times in a minute, with some respondents pausing to question their spelling and others even questioning whether 'door' was a real word at all.

A related phenomenon is *presque-vu*, meaning 'almost seen', which describes the tip-of-the-tongue feeling of almost being able to recall something, while the American comedian George Carlin defined *vujà-dé* as 'the strange feeling that somehow this has never happened before'.]

♦

Forget-me-nots take their name from the tradition that those who wear them will never be forgotten by their lovers.

♦

Touch-me-not is an old name for *Ecballium elaterium* – the 'exploding cucumber' – so-called because it bursts open when touched.

♦

To *explode* originally meant 'to jeer a performer from the stage'.

♦

Exsibilation is the collective booing and hissing of an angry audience.

♦

A *heckler* was originally someone who combed and smoothed flax.

Unkempt literally means 'uncombed'.

A group of barbers is called a *loquacity*.

Barber, *rebarbative* and *Barbados* all derive from the Latin word for 'beard'.

In Old English, a *frumberdling* was a young boy growing in his first beard.

A *beard second* is a unit of 5 nanometres – or the length a beard grows in one second.

The act of trimming or shaving a beard is *pogonotomy*. The process of growing a beard is *pogonotrophy*. A treatise written on the subject of beards is a *pogonology*.

The *pogonion* is the foremost point of the chin.

Sobriquet derives from a French word meaning 'hit under the chin'.

The toast *chin-chin* is apparently derived from the Chinese salutation *ts'ing-ts'ing*.

The phrase 'when you are eating grapes you don't spit out the skin, but when you are not eating grapes you do spit out the skin' is a tongue-twister in Chinese.

The *uvula*, the fleshy hanging protuberance at the back of the throat, means 'little grape' in Latin.

The *Adam's apple* takes its name from a story in which part of the forbidden fruit became stuck in Adam's throat as he swallowed it.

The adjective *adamless* means 'entirely inhabited by women'.

Spanandry is a scarcity of men in a population.

Amazonism is a nineteenth-century word for any situation in which women have all the control.

Amazon is said to mean 'without breasts'.

[Long before the greatest river in the world (no, not the Tyne) was known to Europeans, the name *Amazon* was that of a band of tough female warriors who were supposed to inhabit Scythia, the great unexplored region of Eurasia lying north and east of the Black Sea. The exact meaning of the name *Amazon* is unclear, but popular etymology claims that the warriors had the no-nonsense habit of removing one of their breasts (*mazos* in Greek) so that they could stretch their bows back to their fullest while hunting or fighting.

This remained the only meaning of *Amazon* for another 2,000 years, until the Spanish explorer and conquistador Francisco de Orellana travelled to South America and, in 1541, sailed the full length of the Amazon – then known somewhat less snappily as the Rio Santa Maria de la Mar Dulce. Along the way, Orellana and his men were attacked by a band of native Tapuya women (or, as some later historians claim, a group of long-haired men), whom they referred to as 'Amazons'.]

♦

Jacket derives via French and Spanish from *sakk*, the Arabic word for 'breastplate'.

♦

Straitjackets were originally called 'strait-waistcoats'.

♦

The word *straitlaced* literally refers to the tightly tied laces of a corset.

♦

Bootlaces were once called *boot-whangs*.

♦

A *whangdoodle* was originally the name of a mythical creature mentioned in a satirical sermon in the mid-nineteenth century.

[In 1855, a sermon called 'Where the Lion Roareth and the Wang-Doodle Mourneth' appeared in a local newspaper in New Orleans. The sermon credited itself to 'a unlarnt Hard-shell Baptist preacher', but was in fact the satirical work of William Penn Brannan, a freelance artist and comic writer who throughout his short life (he died in 1866, aged forty-one) contributed numerous nonsensical tales and burlesque stories to newspapers across America. Brannan's tale of the 'wang-doodle' poked fun both at the Bible's predictions of the 'day of wrath', and the strident fire-and-brimstone preachers of the time, who where all too keen to condemn people's debauchery:

Now my brethering, as I have before told you, I am an oneddicated man, and know nothing of grammar talk and collidge highfalutin, but I am a plane unlarnt preacher of the Gospil, what's been fore-ordaned and called to prepare a pervarse generashun for the day of wrath – ah! 'For they shall gnaw a file, and flee unto the mountains of Hepsidam, whar the lion roareth and the wang-doodle mourneth for his first born' – ah!]

♦

A *gyascutus* is an imaginary creature whose legs are said to be longer on one side than the other, so that it can walk on hillsides.

[Variously known as the *gouger*, the *sidehill*, the *wampahoofus* and the *gwinter* – beside a great many other names in different local legends across America – tales of the legendary *gyascutus* began to appear in New England folklore in the early nineteenth century. Although every region appears to have its own account of the creature's appearance and origins, its unequal legs are a common trait that not only allow it to walk on hillsides, but also infers that 'clockwise' and 'counter-clock-wise' gyascutuses are naturally predisposed to dislike one another, and that in order to move about on level ground two gyascutuses have to cling to one another for support and walk, according to one account dating from 1939, 'like a pair of drunks going home from town'.]

♦

A *chichevache* is a mythical creature said to eat only good, patient women.

[The name *chichevache* is an English corruption (apparently based on the misapprehension that the creature was a cow, or *vache*) of the French *chiche-face*, meaning 'lean' or 'meagre face': the myth implies that due to the scarcity of its prey, the chichevache is constantly hungry and malnourished. Its partner is the *bycorne*, another mythical monster said only to prey on patient, long-suffering husbands – and so it is always portrayed as being grossly overfed.

The pair originated in French folklore during the Dark Ages but were adopted into English by writers like Geoffrey Chaucer, who mentioned the chichevache in his *Canterbury Tales*, and John Lydgate, a fifteenth-century poet and friar whose poem, *Bycorne and Chychevache* (circa 1430), explains of the unfortunate creature:

Ful scarce, God wot, is hir vitayle,
Humble wyves she fyndethe so fewe,
For alweys at the countretayle
Theyre tunge clappithe and dothe hewe[.]
[*So scarce, God knows, is her victual,*
Humble wives she finds so few,
For always in reply
Their tongues clap and hew[.]]]

♦

The American lexicographer Noah Webster suggested that *women* should be spelled 'wimmen'.

[Noah Webster's *Compendious Dictionary of the English Language* (1806) was the first true dictionary of purely American English, and in it Webster took the opportunity to implement a series of innovative spelling reforms that he saw as a means of simplifying and improving the language. Under his direction, *colour* and *humour* came to be spelled *color* and *humor*; *plough* simplified to *plow*; *centre* was rearranged to *center*; *cancelled* and *travelled* lost their extraneous Ls and became *canceled* and *traveled*; and the final Ks of *musick* and *publick* were lost, just as they had been in British English a century earlier. Webster continued to wield the axe (or rather the *ax*) on other words, but not all of his suggestions hit the mark – despite calling 'wimmen' the 'old and true spelling' of *women*, it was never adopted. Likewise his suggestions that *ache* should be spelled 'ake', that *daughter* should become 'dawter', *rein* and *reindeer* should become 'rane' and 'ranedeer', and *tongue* should 'more correctly' be spelled 'tung' were all widely ignored. Nevertheless, many of the reforms and suggestions that Webster introduced still divide American and British English to this day.]

◆

St Lucia is the only country named after a woman.

[The Caribbean republic of St Lucia was named by French colonists in honour of St Lucy of Syracuse, a third-century Italian saint who was martyred during the Roman Emperor Diocletian's persecution of Christians in 304 AD. No other independent country in the world today is named after a woman: St Helena in the South Atlantic is a British Overseas Territory not an independent country, and even if gods and goddesses are included the only other contenders are probably *Éire*, the Irish name for the Republic of Ireland, which comes from the name of the Gaelic goddess Éiru, and Tunisia, which theoretically takes its name from the Phoenician goddess Tanith.]

♦

The earliest use of *Mr Right* to refer to a woman's ideal
partner dates from 1796.

[The English writer John Crane – writing under the pseudonym 'A bird
at Bromsgrove' – apparently coined the term *Mr Right* in his 1796 poem
'An Address To Bachelors':

The Maids, poor things, are not to blame […]
Held to a Spark the match would light,
And only wait for Mr Right.]

♦

The French equivalent of 'mister', *monsieur*, was
originally the title held by the eldest brother of the King
of France.

♦

Dauphin, the title held by the eldest son of the king of
France, literally means 'dolphin'.

♦

A *delphinestrian* is someone who rides on the back of a
dolphin.

♦

Porpoise literally means 'pork-fish'.

♦

The French equivalent of 'to have other fish to fry' – *avoir d'autres chats à fouetter* – means 'to have other cats to whip'.

♦

James Joyce used the word *mrkgnao* for the sound of a cat's miaow.

♦

In Japanese, a cat sitting with all of its paws held under its body is called *kobako-zuwari* – meaning 'sitting like an incense box'.

♦

A *cat's carriage* or *king's cushion* is a 'seat' made by two people interlocking their hands so as to lift up a third.

♦

In the 1600s, a *cushion-thumper* was a violent preacher who would beat his hands while delivering sermons.

♦

A *titivil* is a devil supposed to collect the dropped or mispronounced words and curse words of a congregation and carry them back to Hell.

♦

Lalochezia is the use of foul language to relieve stress or cope with pain.

♦

Fuck wasn't included in any major English dictionary from 1795 until 1965.

[*Fuck* wasn't always considered as ignominious a word as it is today: in the 1600s and 1700s, for instance, kestrels were fairly uncompromisingly nicknamed *fuckwinds*. But criticism and censorship of all foul language, no matter how opprobrious, soon took over and Samuel Johnson excluded the word entirely from his dictionary in 1755. Forty years later, the second edition of *A New and Complete Dictionary* (1795) compiled by the English lexicographer (and Baptist minister) John Ash became the last dictionary for another two centuries to sully its pages with the F-word, which Ash described as 'a low vulgar word', meaning 'to perform the act of generation'. The Obscene Publications Act finally outlawed the use of *fuck* in print in the UK in 1857, but was powerless to prevent its use in spoken English. Unrestricted, the use of *fuck* in First World War slang and bawdy wartime ballads, as well as its defiant appearances in the works of authors like James Joyce (*Ulysses*, 1922), D. H. Lawrence (*Lady Chatterley's Lover*, 1928) and Henry Miller (*Tropic of Cancer*, 1934), all prompted the 1965 edition of the *Penguin English Dictionary* to end the taboo once and for all after 170 years of censorship.]

♦

Comstockery is the excessive censorship of literature or art.

[Anthony Comstock was a nineteenth-century American moral crusader, much of whose life was spent tackling obscenity and upholding morality and decency. The founder of the New York Society for the Suppression of Vice (which famously landed the actress Mae West with ten days in prison in 1927 by lobbying her Broadway stageshow, *Sex*), in 1873 Comstock successfully petitioned Congress to introduce a severe set of directives – nicknamed 'Comstock Law' – that made it an offence to deliver 'obscene, lewd or lascivious' material through the US Postal Service. Although primarily concerned with pornography, Comstock's definition of 'lewd or lascivious' material apparently included everything from birth control literature to anatomy textbooks. For all of his efforts as a self-styled 'weeder in God's garden', *Comstockery* was coined in a *New York Times* editorial in 1895.

Ten years later, when George Bernard Shaw's controversial play *Mrs Warren's Profession* (1894) fell foul of the Comstock Laws on its Broadway premiere in 1905, Shaw labelled *Comstockery* 'the world's standing joke at the expense of the United States', which made America appear 'a second-rate, country-town civilisation'. Comstock, in response, labelled Shaw 'an Irish smut dealer'.]

◆

A string of random symbols and punctuation marks used to censor swearwords – like 'f@#?!' – is called a *grawlix*.

◆

An *interrobang* ‽ is a combined question mark and exclamation mark.

[Like the *punctus percontativus*, the *interrobang*, ‽, is another potentially useful but criminally underused punctuation mark. It was the brainchild of Martin K. Speckter, an American advertising executive and typographer, who introduced it in his magazine *Type Talks* in 1962, arguing:

[…] we don't know exactly what Columbus had in mind when he shouted 'Land, ho.' Most historians insist that he cried, 'Land, ho!' but there are others who claim it was really 'Land ho?'. Chances are the intrepid Discoverer was both excited and doubtful, but neither at that time did we, nor even yet, do we, have a point which clearly combines and melds interrogation with exclamation.

Speckter was initially unsure what to call his invention and suggested the name *interrobang* alongside 'exclamaquest', before opening the debate up to readers. They happily contributed their own suggestions, including 'excloragative', 'interrapoint', and 'rhet', but *interrobang* was the only name that stuck. Nevertheless, it sadly remains something of a rarity in English literature.]

♦

Saint-Louis-du-Ha! Ha! in Quebec is the only place name in the world containing two exclamation marks.

[The village of Westward Ho! in Devon is renowned for its singular use of an exclamation mark (taken from an 1855 Charles Kingsley novel), but in comparison Canada's Saint-Louis-du-Ha! Ha! makes it look relatively normal. In this case, the *Ha! Ha!* is actually a ha-ha, an old word for a sunken ditch or moat intended not to be visible until you're right upon it, which in its native French was once used of any obstacle that blocks your path. In the case of Saint-Louis-du-Ha! Ha!, this obstacle is thought to be the nearby Lake Témiscouata, a 45 km-long waterway that presumably thwarted the settlers and explorers who established the town in the nineteenth century.]

♦

According to the Domestic Names Committee of the United States Board on Geographic Names, only five places in the entire USA are permitted to contain a possessive apostrophe.

[Since it was founded in 1890, the USBGN has sought to discourage the use of possessive apostrophes in American place names. Although the Board's reasoning was never officially made clear, it's presumed the move was an attempt either to standardise geographical spellings across America, or else to avoid becoming embroiled in quarrels over ownership of the land – although one popular theory claims the practice was simply intended to avoid apostrophes being misinterpreted as rocks on maps. Whatever the reason, the USBGN has only permitted five possessive apostrophes in its history, namely those in Martha's Vineyard, Massachusetts (after a rigorous local campaign in 1933); Ike's Point, New Jersey (1944, because it would be 'unrecognisable otherwise'); John E's Pond, Rhode Island (1963, so as to avoid it being misread as 'John S Pond'); Carlos Elmer's Joshua View, Arizona (1995, because 'otherwise three apparently given names in succession would dilute the meaning'); and Clark's Mountain, Oregon (2002, in deference to North American explorers Lewis and Clark).]

✦

Apostrophe means 'turning away' in Greek.

✦

A right angle or a 90° turn can also be called a *hemisemiperigon*.

✦

When written in upper-case letters, the word SWIMS is the longest English word that is still legible when rotated 180°.

[A word or symbol that can be read upside-down – or else intentionally reads something different when turned upside-down – is known as an *ambigram*, and *SWIMS* is reportedly the longest example in the English language. Shorter examples include *MOW*, *pod* and *suns*, although the six-letter word *dollop* would steal the crown were it not for its lower case Ls falling below the line when turned upside-down.]

In the US army, a *double time* march should specifically comprise 180 steps of 36 inches per minute.

♦

To *trigintisextuple* means 'to multiply by thirty-six'.

♦

In American surveying, a *township* is a precise unit of area equal to thirty-six square miles.

> [Survey townships were introduced in America by the Homestead Act of 1862. They formed the basis of the so-called 'land rushes' of the late nineteenth century, which opened up previously unavailable lands to settlers looking to colonise the central United States. One *township* was defined as a square of six-by-six survey miles, divided into thirty-six square-mile *sections*, each of which in turn comprised four *quarter-sections* of 160 acres, and sixteen *quarter-quarter-sections* of forty acres. Most land rushes allocated one quarter-section plot to each settler, often on a first-come-first-serve basis.]

♦

A measurement of ⅓₆ of a foot, or one-third of an inch, is called a *barleycorn*.

♦

Barley-fumble is an old Scots word for a truce or a call to end a game.

♦

A *finger-fumbler* – like the phrase 'good blood, bad blood' – is the sign language equivalent of a tongue-twister.

◆

'Natasha did not tie up her cat Pacha, who escaped' – *Natacha n'attacha pas son chat Pacha qui s'échappa* – is a tongue-twister in French.

◆

Catgut has nothing to do with cats. A *light year* isn't a unit of time. *Tidal waves* aren't tidal. *Silkworms* aren't worms.

[The 'cat' of *catgut* is believed to have originally been 'kit', the name of a small fiddle dating from the Middle Ages. The 'gut' of *catgut*, however, is the same as in *guts* – the strings of violins and similar instruments were once made from sheep intestines.

Despite their name, *light years* are units of distance, not time, and refer to the distance that light – moving at 299,792,458 metres per second – travels in one year. As such, one light year is a distance of approximately 9.4×10^{12} km (5.9×10^{12} miles), or just under ten trillion kilometres.

The name *tidal wave* was originally applied to the highest high-water wave that accompanied and was caused by a high tide. In the mid-nineteenth century, however, it came to be used erroneously of a tsunami (literally 'harbour wave' in Japanese), which is caused by an underwater earthquake and so has nothing to do with the tide at all. Before then, incidentally, what we might call a tidal wave today had been known as a *watershake*.

Silkworms, lastly, aren't worms but caterpillars – the larval stage of the *Bombyx* moth native to south-east Asia. Likewise, *inchworms* and *cutworms* are also caterpillars, while *glow-worms*, *woodworms* and *mealworms* are all beetle larvae. Perhaps most misleading of all, however, is the *slowworm* or *blindworm*, which, despite its name and remarkably snake-like appearance, is in fact a legless lizard.]

♦

The word *vermin* literally only applies to worms.

[*Vermin* – like *vermicelli* – is a derivative of the Latin word for 'worm', *vermis*, and in the sense of 'objectionable creatures' probably originally referred to caterpillars or maggots, which could devastate crops and render food uneatable.]

♦

Slugs were originally called *dew-snails*.

♦

Slug-nuttiness is punch-drunkenness – the dazed or stupefied sensation caused by a blow to the head.

♦

Head-Smashed-In Buffalo Jump is a World Heritage Site in Canada.

[A *buffalo jump* is a cliff or precipice once used by the Native Americans to hunt bison, which they would drive over the edge in vast numbers. Head-Smashed-In Buffalo Jump in Alberta is one of the most notable examples in all of North America and is known to have been used by local tribes intermittently for almost 6,000 years. Its name apparently comes from a legend amongst the Blackfoot tribesmen, one of whom was apparently so keen to watch the events of a buffalo hunt that he stood directly beneath the clifftop and was crushed to death as the herd were cajoled over the edge.]

♦

A *cañada* is a small canyon.

♦

Canyon, *cannon* and *cannelloni* all derive from the Latin word for a pipe.

♦

Pipe dreams were originally the fantastic visions a person saw while smoking opium.

♦

The Greek word for opium extract, *meconium*, is also the medical name for a newborn baby's first bowel movement.

♦

Genuine comes from the Latin word for 'knee', *genu*, and refers to the practice of a father cradling a newborn son or daughter on his knee to acknowledge his paternity.

♦

A *penanggalan* is a female vampire that preys on newborn babies.

> [The monstrous *penanggalan* derives from Malaysian folklore, in which she is described as a disembodied head – often depicted with her stomach and entrails hanging below – that flies from village to village attaching herself to childbearing mothers, and feeding off their newborn babies. According to one tale, the *penanggalan* was born from a lascivious woman who was trying to catch the attention of some passing men outside her window, but when her husband noticed and

tried to pull her back inside, her head detached itself from her body and flew away.]

♦

Dracula means 'son of the dragon' in Romanian.

♦

Dragoons are so-called because they were originally armed with a 'dragon', a firearm that supposedly 'breathed fire' when it was shot.

♦

Blunderbuss derives from the Dutch for 'thunder-box'.

♦

Blunderkin, *batie-bum*, *fog-pate* and *shaffles* are all old names for foolish or easily confused people.

♦

A pair of lines of text with identical or easily confused endings is called a *homoeoteleuton*.

> [In rhetoric, a *homoeoteleuton* is a figure of speech that repeats the same or similar words at the end of subsequent lines or clauses, to memorable effect:
>
> > [...] my mother weeping, my father wailing, my sister crying, our maid howling, our cat wringing her hands, and all our house in a great perplexity[.]
> >
> > — *The Two Gentlemen of Verona* (II.iii)
>
> In more general use, however, *homoeoteleuton* describes a mistake made in reading or writing caused by two adjacent lines of text having similar

endings or containing similar words. Long before the days of the printing press, this kind of error could prove disastrous to scribes and copyists as they painstakingly copied out their books and other documents, who risked missing out swathes of text if their eye happened to jump inadvertently from one word on a page to the same word elsewhere. A famous example of precisely that comes from the Old Testament Book of Samuel:

> Then Nahash the Ammonite came up, and encamped against Jabeshgilead: and all the men of Jabesh said unto Nahash, Make a covenant with us, and we will serve thee. And Nahash the Ammonite answered them, On this condition will I make a covenant with you, that I may thrust out all your right eyes, and lay it for a reproach upon all Israel.

> — 1 Samuel 11:1–2

As it is, the Bible offers no explanation as to why Nahash should, apparently unprovoked, want to blind 'all the men of Jabesh', and for centuries biblical scholars were left with little recourse other than to believe he was probably just having a bad day. That was until the Dead Sea Scrolls were discovered in the 1940s and 50s, which showed that a scribal error had caused the text to leap ahead from one appearance of 'Nahash' to another, missing out a chunk of the original text. Recent editions of the Bible have since restored the missing verse, which explains that the blinded men in question were all rebels and insurgents who had earlier escaped Nahash's bloody persecution of 'the Gadites and the Reubenites', which had left 'no one … across the Jordan whose right eye Nahash, king of the Ammonites, had not gouged out'. Nahash, it seems, was just catching up on unfinished business.]

◆

A pair of railway lines crossing over one another in an X shape is called a *diamond-point*.

◆

The tiny waste fragments and shavings left over when a diamond is cut are called *bort*. It means 'bastard' in Old French.

♦

Bastard derives from the French *fils de bast*, meaning 'pack-saddle son'. It literally refers to a child conceived on a makeshift bed made from a horse's saddle.

♦

A *batman* was originally the member of a military convoy who was in charge of the *bât-horse* – the horse that carried all of the officers' baggage on its saddle.

♦

The first city ever nicknamed *Gotham* was Newcastle upon Tyne.

> [In Tudor English, *Gothamists* or *Gothamites* were proverbial fools. Their name apparently derives from a long-lost ballad or folktale that recounted 'three wise men of Gotham', who in the course of the story seemingly did little else besides make idiots of themselves. In this context, Gotham was portrayed as a backwater rural village (perhaps fictional, but identified by some sources as 'Gotham-hall' in Essex) whose rustic inhabitants were likely the butt of many a joke amongst the more sophisticated and urbane Londoners nearby.
>
> As time went by, the name *Gotham* came to be applied to any town whose inhabitants were seen as being similarly unsophisticated or uncultured, and it was probably in this sense that it came (entirely unfairly, of course) to be attached to Newcastle upon Tyne around 1800. Once there however, *Gotham* appears to have lost its negative connotations and become a local nickname for the city itself: *A Glossary*

of North Country Words recorded in 1825 that *Gotham* was already 'a Cant name for Newcastle', but even earlier than that the name was used in a local folksong, *Kiver Awa'*, written in 1804:

Heav'n prosper thee, Gotham! thou famous old town,
Of the Tyne the chief glory and pride:
May thy heroes acquire immortal renown,
In the dread field of Mars when they're try'd.

For *Kiver Awa'* to make sense, *Gotham* has presumably to have been in local use earlier than 1804, but even as it stands this song predates the earliest record of New York being called 'Gotham City' by four years.]

♦

Geordie is derived from the name 'George'.

[Admittedly no one is entirely sure why Newcastle natives are called *Geordies*, and the only solid fact appears to be that the nickname is derived from a pet form of 'George'. Precisely which George this alludes to is another matter, with suspects ranging from George II (the north-east of England was a royalist stronghold during the Jacobite Rebellion), to the general use of 'George' to mean 'bloke' or 'man', as 'Jack' or 'John' might be used today. Perhaps the most popular theory, however, claims that the George in question is George Stephenson, the engineer and figurehead of the Industrial Revolution who was born in Wylam, ten miles west of Newcastle, in 1781. Stephenson opened his first workshop in the city in the early 1800s, and in 1815 invented a new type of miner's lamp which was soon dubbed 'the Geordie lamp'.]

♦

George means 'earth-worker' in Greek. It's derived from the same root as words like *geography* and *geology*.

♦

The *Oxford English Dictionary*'s entry for the word *set* is twice as long as George Orwell's *Animal Farm*.

> [Until it was surpassed by *run* in 2011, the word *set* had the most definitions in the *Oxford English Dictionary* – a total, according to the *Guinness Book of Records*, of 430. Its full dictionary entry currently runs to some 60,000 words, equivalent to two *Animal Farms* (which reaches a paltry 29,900); two *Charlie and the Chocolate Factories* (at 30,600 each); one *Lord of the Flies* (62,500); a *Mrs Dalloway* (63,000); half a *Sense and Sensibility* (119,000); or roughly a ninth of *War and Peace* (544,000).]

♦

In American slang, a *farmer's haircut* is one that leaves a visible line of pale skin between the hairline and the tanned back of the neck.

♦

An *acersecomic* person is someone whose hair has never been cut.

♦

Comet derives from the Greek *aster kometes*, literally meaning 'long-haired star'.

♦

In the early 1900s, a *long-hair* was someone with an interest in classical music.

♦

First described in 1993, the *Mozart effect* is a temporary increase in mental ability caused by listening to classical music.

♦

The *Alec* of 'smart Alec' is said to be a mid-nineteenth-century New York pickpocket called Aleck Hoag.

♦

In the sixteenth century, pickpockets were called *fig-boys*.

♦

Sycophant derives from the Greek for 'fig-shower'.

♦

To give someone the fig is a derisive gesture made by pushing the thumb through two of the closed fingers of the hand.

> [They mightn't seem like it, but *sycophancy* and *giving the fig* are actually related to one another. Making a 'fig' with your thumb was apparently a common means of showing your contempt in Ancient Greece, and although the politicians of the time would naturally rise above making such lewd gestures – thereby allowing them to sycophantically ingrati-ate themselves with their opponents – in private, they encouraged their supporters to heckle and taunt them.]

♦

Thumb, thimble, nimble and *limb* were all originally spelled without a B.

> [These four words were spelled *þuma, þymel, næmel* and *lim* in Old

English, and their extraneous Bs didn't begin to emerge until the early Middle Ages. They're all examples of a language phenomenon called *epenthesis*, in which an additional sound is unintentionally added to a word to bridge a gap between the two sounds either side of it: try saying an *mmm* sound and an *lll* sound quickly, one after the other, and you'll soon see how easily a *b* can materialise between them.

Epenthesis is the same phenomenon that accounts for the D in *thunder* (*thunor* in Old English), the N in *passenger* (which comes from the French *passager*), and the B in *hombre* (which, like *human*, comes from the Latin *homine*), and it even explains the extra sounds that creep into careless pronunciations of words like *hamPster*, *athUHlete*, and *warmPth*.]

♦

The phrase *humble pie* derives from *umbles*, an old name for the innards of an animal.

♦

Frisbees were originally made out of pie tins from Mrs Frisbie's Bakery in Bridgeport, Connecticut.

♦

Allen keys are named after the Allen Manufacturing Company in Hartford, Connecticut.

♦

The Japanese word for 'stapler', *hocchikisu*, derives from the staplers manufactured at the EH Hotchkiss Company in Norwalk, Connecticut.

♦

A native of Connecticut is called a *Nutmegger*.

♦

Nutmeg, *hornswoggle*, *honeyfuggle* and *coney-catch* all mean to trick or deceive someone.

> [In games like football, basketball and hockey, incidentally, a *nutmeg* is a
> technique in which a player passes the ball through an opponent's legs
> and then quickly regains it on the other side.]

♦

A *wagpastie* is a roguish, unprincipled person.

♦

An *illywhacker* is a confidence trickster.

♦

In the fifteenth century, *evil-willy* meant 'malevolent', or 'wishing harm on others'.

♦

The Latin equivalent of 'willy-nilly' was *nolens volens*. It literally means 'unwilling willing'.

♦

Shilly-shally is a corruption of 'shall I, shall I'.

♦

Rusty-fusty is an old name for the stale air and dust that accumulates in a closed room.

◆

Higgledy-piggledy is an example of a *sdrucciola* rhyme, in which the final three syllables of a pair of words or lines of poetry all rhyme.

[In poetry, masculine rhymes are those in which only the final stressed syllables in a pair of lines of verse rhyme with one another – as in William Blake's 'Tyger! Tyger! Burning *bright* / In the forest of the *night*'. In feminine rhymes, there are two final rhyming syllables, only the first of which is stressed – as in 'Once upon a midnight *dreary*, when I pondered weak and *weary*', the opening line of Edgar Allan Poe's 'The Raven'. A *sdrucciola* rhyme, however, involves three syllables with the stress falling on the third from last, a pattern that produces lively and memorable couplets like *vanity / sanity*, *venerate / generate*, and *higgledy-piggledy*. Rhyming pairs of polysyllabic words like these, however, are relatively scarce in English, and as such writers employing sdrucciola rhymes in their work are often required to manipulate the language in highly ingenious and bizarre ways. One famous example comes from Ogden Nash's nonsense poem 'The Axolotl':

I've never met an axolotl,
But Harvard has one in a bottle,
Perhaps – and at the thought I shiver –
The very villain from Fall River,
Where Lizzie Borden took an axolotl
And gave her mother forty whaxolotl.

Sdrucciola, appropriately enough, means 'slippery' in Italian.]

◆

An *anapaest* is a word or metrical foot comprised of three syllables, two short and one long – like *contradict* or *volcano*.

Lava means 'washes' in Italian. *Magma* means 'dregs' in Latin.

♦

There is a specific type of lava flow called an *aa*.

♦

Eeee ee ee means 'she will eat it' in Manx.

♦

The proper name for 'eating your words' is *autologophagy*.

♦

An *autological* word is one that describes itself, like 'readable', 'grandiloquent' or 'unhyphenated'. A *heterological* word is one that doesn't describe itself, like 'long', 'misspelled' or 'monosyllabic'.

♦

There are only five monosyllabic countries in the world. Three of them are in Europe.

[The five countries in question are France, Spain, Greece, Chad and Laos (which despite appearances should rhyme with *cow*, not *chaos*). If Wales is included, this total rises to six – with four of the six located in Europe.]

♦

One theory claims that *Europe* is derived from a Greek word meaning 'wide-faced'.

♦

Prosopagnosia is the inability to recognise faces.

♦

Anyone who is *aspectabund* has a particularly expressive face.

♦

In Puerto Rican Spanish, 'to have a face like a busy telephone' – *tener una cara de telefono ocupado* – means 'to be very angry'.

♦

Besides *angry* and *hungry*, English words ending in —*gry* include *aggry*, a type of bead; *iggry*, an old slang word meaning 'hurry up'; and *conyngry*, an old name for a rabbit warren.

> [Asking someone to name a third English word ending in —*gry* is a popular word puzzle, and it's an equally popular misconception to claim that there are no other —*gry* words in English. While it's certainly fair to say that *angry* and *hungry* are the only two common examples, the English language being what it is, they certainly aren't the only ones. Besides those listed here, the *Oxford English Dictionary* also lists *higry-pigry*, a purgative drug; *podagry*, an old name for the gouty condition podagra, and the name of a climbing plant; and several clumsy and rarely-used derivatives like *unangry* and *anhungry*, meaning 'in a state of hunger'. Even *gry* itself is a word in its own right, which as well

as being used as a verb meaning 'to roar', is the name of an obscure measurement equal to ⅟₁₀₀ of an inch.]

♦

Bunny derives from an old word for a squirrel not a rabbit.

[*Bunny* is a derivative of *bun*, which as far back as the early sixteenth century was being used in English as a pet name for all kinds of furry creatures. Its earliest record, however, comes from *The Worthiness of Wales* (1587), a poem by Thomas Churchyard, which refers to the pet squirrel of a tragic young woman:

> They say her squirrell lept away,
> And toward it she run:
> And as from a fall she sought to stay
> The little pretie Bun,
> Right downe from top of wall she fell,
> And tooke her death thereby.

Churchyard – a favourite of Elizabeth I, until she took offence at one of his earlier works – dedicated this poem to the queen in an attempt to regain her approval, and she was impressed enough to award the seventy-three-year-old writer a comfortable pension. It may have won over the Queen of England, but later critics were less keen:

> Whether the republisher of this piece of linsey-wolsey be a Welchman ... we know not. But, if it were not to commemorate the worthiness of Wales, it might as well, for the worth of the Poem, as it is called, have been buried in a Church-yard with the bones of its author.
>
> — *The London Review of English and Foreign Literature* (1776)]

♦

In Australian slang, anything described as *beyond the rabbit-proof fence* is extremely remote, or lies away from civilisation.

◆

Boondocks, meaning 'outskirts' or 'wilds', was borrowed into English from Tagalog, the official language of the Philippines.

> [*Boondocks* has been used to refer to rough or remote country in American slang since the early 1900s (while *boondockers* are shoes suitable for wearing in the boondocks). The word comes from the Tagalog for 'mountain', *bundok*, and was probably first adopted into English during the American occupation of the Philippines in the decades leading up to the Second World War.]

◆

The *wilder–* of 'wilderness' literally means 'wild deer'.

◆

The Croatian word for September, *rujan*, means 'deer-mating month'.

◆

In American politics, an *October surprise* is an event arranged immediately before an election in order to win over the electorate.

◆

Psephology is the study of elections.

♦

Gerrymandering – rigging an election by rearranging the electorate – is named after Massachusetts Governor Elbridge Gerry.

> [In 1812, Governor Elbridge Gerry passed a bill that redrew the Massachusetts electoral district borders so that they would favour his Democratic–Republican Party. The ploy worked, and the senate remained in his party's hands. Although the practice of *gerrymandering* is much older (the Anti-Federalist leader Patrick Henry tried the same trick in Virginia in 1788, to scupper James Madison's election to Congress) it is Gerry who has earned his place in the dictionary thanks to an article in the *Boston Globe* on 26 March 1812 that likened the shape of one of his redrawn districts to that of a salamander. The *gerrymander*, as it was called (which, like the Governor's surname, should really begin with a hard *g* not a *j* sound), was born.]

♦

Grangerizing – a reader illustrating their own book – is named after the English historian James Granger.

> [James Granger's *Biographical History of England* (1769) contained several pages that had been left blank so that readers could collect and supply their own illustrations. His clever idea proved hugely successful, and 'grangerising' books became a popular hobby in eighteenth- and nineteenth-century England]

♦

Fletcherising – chewing your food at least thirty times before swallowing – is named after US health food enthusiast Horace Fletcher.

> [If you're going to be remembered by a nickname, it's fair to say

'The Great Masticator' probably wouldn't be your first choice. Nevertheless, it's by this particular moniker that the American lifestyle guru Horace Fletcher came to be known in the early 1900s. Throughout his life Fletcher advocated a number of nutritional techniques and outlined various theories and instructions in print, all of which conspired to make 'Fletcherism' one of the foremost diet plans of its time – and made its inventor a very wealthy man. Amongst his many philosophies, Fletcher encouraged never eating when angry or worried; never eating after 7 p.m.; chewing drinks, and holding them in your mouth for thirty seconds before swallowing; and always examining your faeces (or 'digestion-ash' as he euphemistically called it), which he advised 'should be quite dry, having only the odour of moist clay or of a hot biscuit'. Above all else, however, chewing – or 'munching' as he preferred to call it – was the key to good digestion, and *fletcherising* your food with at least thirty chews was best:

> Starchy foods, such as bread, potatoes, etc., require from thirty to seventy masticatory movements to assist saliva to turn the starch into 'grape sugar', which is the form in which it can be used as nourishment. You will at once think, no doubt, that a range of numbers extending from thirty to seventy is pretty wide. So it is; but conditions regarding the qualities of not only breads, but potatoes, and also conditions relative to the strength or supply of saliva, differ greatly.

> — *Fletcherism: What It Is* (1913), Horace Fletcher]

♦

Chankings are the inedible parts of certain foods, like bones or seeds, that are spat out while eating.

♦

A *spit-poison* is an overly malicious or spiteful person.

♦

Before it came to be used of a sharp or noticeable flavour, a *tang* was the part of a snake's tongue where its venom was supposedly found.

♦

The first thing ever referred to as having a *flavour of the month* was ice cream.

♦

The Estonian word for the edge of an area of ice is *jäääär*.

♦

An *aquabob* is an icicle.

♦

Ice legs are the equivalent of *sea legs* – a person's ability to keep their balance on ice.

♦

Samuel Johnson's *Dictionary* defines a *lizard* as 'an animal resembling a serpent, with legs added to it'.

♦

Bootlegging derives from the practice of nineteenth-century smugglers trafficking illicit bottles of alcohol in their boots.

♦

The part of a sock that covers the foot is called the *vamp*. It comes from an Old French word, *avanpié*, meaning 'in front of the foot'.

♦

A *pediscript* is a piece of text written using your feet instead of your hands.

♦

If your second toe is longer than your big toe, then you have a *Greek foot*, or *Morton's toe*.

♦

Tick-tack-toe was once called *tip-tap-toe*. Rock-paper-scissors was once called *ick-ack-ock*. Tag was once called *widdy-widdy-way*.

♦

A *waywiser* is an instrument used to measure a distance travelled.

♦

A *mileway* is a period of twenty minutes – or the length of time it takes to walk one mile.

♦

A *ghurry* is one-sixtieth of a day – or precisely twenty-four minutes.

[In Indian English, a *ghurry* or *ghuree* is a type of water clock comprised of a bowl, floating in a basin of water, which slowly fills up through a hole or series of holes in its sides, and sinks to the bottom in precisely twenty-four minutes. This steady process was once used as a means not only of timekeeping, but also of accurately dividing the day into sixty twenty-four-minute sections:

> In summer, when the sun rises about 12 minutes after 5, and sets at 48 after 6, the day is 34 ghurees in length, and the night only 26 … The last ghuree of the day will occasionally be lengthened or shortened, in order to finish the day at sunset, and the last of the night altered in the same way, that the day may begin at sunrise.
>
> — *The New-York Annual Register* (1837)]

♦

Twenty-four is considered an unlucky number in China because it's almost identical to 'easy to die' in Cantonese.

[An aversion or avoidance of the number four – dubbed *tetraphobia* – is common to many East Asian cultures and countries due to the widespread similarity between the words for 'four' and 'death' or 'die' in a number of local languages, including Cantonese, Japanese, Vietnamese and Korean. This alone is often enough to deter drivers from buying cars with fours in their number plates, and even to lower rental prices on the fourth floor of buildings, which are often renamed '3A' or 'D', or else omitted entirely.

In Cantonese especially, this superstition goes on to include all numbers containing a four, including fourteen (which sounds like 'must die') and twenty-four ('easy to die'), all the way up to 9413 – which can be interpreted as meaning 'nine will die, only one will live'.]

♦

One theory claims *kibosh* derives from the Irish *cie báis* or 'cap of death' worn by executioners.

[English speakers have been putting an end to things by *putting a kibosh on* them since the early nineteenth century; the word's earliest known record comes from Dickens's *Sketches By Boz* in 1836. The theory that *kibosh* derives from the Irish *cie báis*, or *caidhp bháis*, is usually said to refer to an executioner's cap, but it could just as plausibly refer to the mask worn by a hanged man, the black cap donned by a judge when handing out a death sentence, or to a cloth placed respectfully over a dead person's face. Alternatively, *kibosh* might be a Yiddish or Hebrew expression, in which case it's often said to derive from a Hebrew word meaning 'eighteen pence', perhaps in the sense of an insultingly trivial sum of money. Some relatively more outlandish theories point to the Arabic *qurbash* (a rhinoceros-hide whip), the Scots *kye-boots* (shackles or fetters worn by cattle), the old German *kiebe* (meaning 'carrion'), and even an old heraldic term, *caboched* (meaning 'cut off at the neck'). But perhaps the neatest explanation is that the '–bosh' of *kibosh* is nothing more than an English slang word for a stout punch or blow, while the initial *'ki–'* simply provides emphasis, as in similarly evocative words like *kerplunk*, *kaboom* and *kersplat*. Whatever its true origin might be *kibosh* remains a tantalising etymological mystery.]

♦

A jester's hat was originally called a *cockscomb*.

♦

A *cock-stride* is a single footstep of a cock, or short and easily walkable distance.

♦

A *passus* was a Roman measurement equal to a single stride – the distance between the back of the heel leaving the ground, to point at which it is set down again.

Heeltap or *alms-drink* is the remnants of a drink left in the bottom of a glass.

♦

A *gulchcup* is someone who drinks a drink down to its last drop.

♦

In Old English, *hiccups* were called *ælfsogoða*, meaning 'elf-chokes'.

♦

In Victorian slang, someone with a loud nagging cough would be called a *member for Berkshire*.

♦

As a slang name for a fool or simpleton, *berk* is derived from the Cockney rhyming slang *Berkshire Hunt*, meaning 'c—t'.

♦

Unterhosenbügler is German slang for 'wimp'. It literally means 'one who irons his underpants'.

> [German has a knack for providing note-perfect compound words to sum up complex feelings or situations, the most famous of which are probably *Schadenfreude*, 'taking pleasure from someone else's misfortune', and *Weltschmerz*, 'a general sentimental sadness' (literally a 'world pain'). Regrettably, English has yet to fully accept the German

concepts of *Spannungsbogen*, 'the excitement-building delay between realising you want something and getting it'; *Anschlusstreffer*, 'a goal scored when 2–0 down which makes the prospect of a draw more likely'; and *Ohrwurm* (literally an 'ear-worm'), a general name for a song that sticks in your head.

It's in insults, though, that German really comes into its own, a fact illustrated by an early twenty-first-century trend in German slang for inventing ever more complicated and evocative compound words that could be used in place of *Weichei*, the German equivalent of 'softie' or 'wimp'. Amongst the first to emerge was *Warmduscher*, 'one who takes warm showers', but this was soon joined by countless others, including *Schattenparker*, 'one who parks their car in the shade'; *Bei-Mami-Wäscher*, 'one who does his laundry at his mother's house'; *Auf-dem-Schrank-Staubwischer*, 'one who dusts on top of the wardrobe'; *Beipackzettel-Leser*, 'one who reads the warning labels on drug prescriptions'; *Vorwärtseinparker*, 'one who drives forwards into a parallel parking space'; and even *Sitzpinkler*, 'one who urinates sitting down'. As well as being an *Unterhosenbügler*, incidentally, you can also be a *Sockenfalter* – 'one who folds his socks'.]

◆

A *skitterbrook* was a coward in seventeenth-century English. It literally means 'someone who shits his breeches'.

◆

Twerp is popularly said to derive from an Oxford University student called T. W. Earp.

[In a letter written to his youngest son, Christopher, on 6 October 1944, the author J. R. R Tolkien recalled 'rooming with [Sir William] Walton the composer', while still a student at Oxford University, 'and going about with T. W. Earp, the original twerp'. There is no doubt at all that Thomas Wade Earp – later a well-regarded art critic, and a good friend also of Dylan Thomas and Augustus John – existed, but despite Tolkien's evidence it remains hotly debated whether he is the genuine origin of *twerp*, or whether his name is nothing more than an unflattering coincidence. Some sources reject Tolkien's explanation altogether and claim instead that *twerp* might date back as far as the mid-nineteenth century, in which case it likely has its roots in some long-lost slang expression. But as it stands, no reliable written record of *twerp* has been found any earlier than 1925, when it first appeared in a dictionary of *Soldier and Sailor Words and Phrases* that defined it as 'an unpleasant person'. T. W. Earp's university studies predate this record by roughly a decade, long enough certainly for his nickname to gain more widespread use – and by all accounts, Earp certainly made enough of a name for himself during his time at Oxford to be remembered long after leaving. According to one tale, when Earp was found passed out in a wheelbarrow full of strawberries at Covent Garden market in 1913, he was sent to a local magistrate's court on a charge of drunk and disorderly behaviour. When asked why he had climbed into the barrow, he replied, 'For valetudinarian reasons, purely valetudinarian reasons'. 'Don't address me as if you were president of the Oxford Union!' the magistrate responded, to which Earp replied simply, 'But I am.']

♦

Conundrum was originally an Oxford University nickname for a pedantic or foolish person.

♦

A *pedant* was originally a schoolteacher.

♦

Schoolmaster is an anagram of 'the classroom'.

Teachers were once known as *lorthews*. It literally means 'teaching-slaves'.

[The first half of the word *lorthew* is the same Old English word, *lore*, as is used today to mean 'knowledge' or 'wisdom'. The second half is an Old English word for 'slave', *þeow*, from which English has gained a handful of equally uncommon terms like *thewdom*, meaning 'slavery' or 'servitude', and *theowten*, meaning 'to serve'. Incidentally, another word for a teacher, *pedagogue*, is another kind of slave: in Ancient Rome, a *paedagogos* was a slave whose job it was to escort Roman children to school each day.]

Ciao is derived from the Italian for 'I am your slave'.

The French word for 'slavery', *esclavage*, is used as the name of a type of necklace in English due to its resemblance to a slave's fetters.

Anodyne necklace, Stolypin's necktie and *John Roper's window* are all old nicknames for a hangman's noose.

The hardest words to guess in a game of hangman are *jazz, buzz, hajj, fuzz* and *jinx*.

[In 2010, the mathematician Jon McLoone used a computer program to simulate fifty games of hangman for all 90,000 words in a dictionary.

These initial rounds narrowed the field down to the thousand trickiest words, and when the program was run again – playing a total of fifteen million games – the hardest word was found to be *jazz*, followed by *buzz*, *hajj* ('a Muslim pilgrimage'), *fuzz*, *jinx*, *fizz*, *puff*, *jiff*, *razz* ('to tease someone'), *buff* and *quiz*. Regardless of how many reprieves the hanged man was allowed (anything from eight to thirteen, depending on how detailed his gallows are made), the toughest words were unsurprisingly characterised by letters like J, Q, X and Z, while four-letter words – and especially words with repeated letters – proved the hardest as they contained fewer guessable letters. Amongst the longer words the program flagged up were *zigzagging*, *beekeepers*, *muzziness*, *parallaxes* and *revivified*.]

◆

Jinx derives from an old English name for the wryneck, a bird of the woodpecker family, which was once widely used in witchcraft.

◆

Mats or tangles of hair found in a horse's mane are nicknamed *witch's stirrups*.

◆

Stirrup literally means 'climbing rope' in Old English.

◆

Someone who climbs over a fence or hedge in order to sneak into a paid event is said to have a *sparrow's ticket*.

◆

Ostrich derives from the Greek for 'big sparrow'.

[*Ostrich* is derived from the Ancient Greek *struthos meagle*, literally meaning 'big sparrow', although the Greeks also knew the ostrich as the *strouthokamelos*, or 'camel-sparrow'. Its earliest reference in English comes from the *Ancrene Riwle*, a thirteenth-century guidebook for anchoresses, which warned women not to give in to their 'flesh and fleshly viceness', which could hold them back just as the ostrich's great bulk keeps it from taking flight:

> The ostrich, on account of its heavy flesh, and other birds like it, try to look as though they are flying and beat their wings; but their feet are constantly dragged to the Earth.]

◆

A male sparrowhawk is called a *musket*.

◆

Muskrats take their name from the Algonquin *musquash*, meaning 'it is red'. *Raccoons* take their name from the Algonquin *arahkunem*, meaning 'he scratches with his hands'.

◆

Caziques, an old name for certain Native American tribal leaders, can score up to 392 points in Scrabble.

[*Caziques* is one of a number of words said under certain circumstances to achieve the highest possible score in a single Scrabble play, alongside other high scorers like *musquash*, *whizbang*, *beziques*, *quixotry* and *quetzals*. To reach 392 points, a player's full rack of seven letters would need to be played around an eighth letter already on the board, so that the Q of *caziques* ends up on a double-letter square, and the initial C and final S are *both* played on triple-word squares. As convoluted as this scenario might seem, other more outlandish theories of what the single highest-scoring Scrabble word could be argue that a player could play all seven of their tiles so as to interlock with eight others already on the board, thereby covering a full row from one side to the other and taking in three triple-word squares along the way. In a highly unlikely (yet theoretically plausible) situation like this, a fifteen-letter word like *benzoxycamphors*, *sesquioxidizing* or *oxyphenbutazone* could earn a player upwards of 1,700 points in a single turn.]

♦

The highest-scoring opening move in a game of Scrabble is *muzjiks*, which can score 128 points.

[*Muzjiks* is an alternative spelling of *muzhiks*, an old sixteenth-century word for Russian peasants or serfs, which as it stands is worth twenty-nine points in standard Scrabble play. Play it on your first go, however, and you'll not only be able to place the Z on a double-letter score, but you'll have your score doubled for playing the first word of the game, and be awarded a bonus of fifty points for using all of your tiles. All in all, you'll earn an impressive 128.]

♦

***Scribble-scrabble*, *pot-hookery* and *griffonage* are all old names for illegible handwriting.**

♦

A person's signature was originally called their *hand-writ*.

♦

The address written on an envelope or above the text of a letter was originally called the *superscription*.

♦

The earliest use of the word *emailed* dates from 1480.
The earliest use of the word *computer* dates from 1613.

> [Needless to say that when 'a longe gowne made of blue clothe of gold upon satyn grounde emaylled' was recorded in the 'wardrobe accounts' of Edward IV in 1480, the writer wasn't talking about email-ing his latest purchase. Unsurprisingly, neither *emailed* nor *computer* meant what they do today when they first appeared in the language in the late Middle Ages: *emailed* meant 'enamelled' (and was derived from the French *émail*), while a *computer* was simply an accountant or number-cruncher – literally 'one who computes'.]

♦

Half of a computer byte is called a *nibble*.

♦

To *nibble-nabble* means 'to do something bit by bit', or 'to act haphazardly'.

♦

A mispronunciation of 'haphazard' is one of the possible origins of the word *half-assed*.

♦

Badassery was added to the *Oxford English Dictionary* in 2013.

♦

Kittiwakes are also known as *tickle-asses*.

♦

Ellis Island in New York was originally called 'Gull Island'.

[Ellis Island in New York Bay was originally called *Kioshk* or 'Gull Island' by the local Lenape Native Americans, but when the Dutch took control in 1630 it was renamed 'Little Oyster Island' in reference to the rich oyster beds that once lined its shores. The name 'Gull Island' was at least partly restored when it fell under British control in the early eighteenth century, but after a band of pirates were hanged there in 1765 it quickly earned the less appealing nickname of 'Gibbet Island'. The modern name 'Ellis Island' dates back to the time of the American Revolution, when a New Yorker named Samuel Ellis acquired the island and attempted to develop it into a local picnic area. His ownership was relatively short-lived however, and after he tried unsuccessfully to sell it in 1785 (by placing an advertisement for 'that pleasant situated island … lying in New York Bay' in a local newspaper), Ellis Island was ceded to the US government in 1808. It was chosen as the site of a new US immigration station in 1890 and remained in use until 1954, during which time more than twelve million American immigrants were processed there.]

♦

A *gully-gully man* is a conjuror who performs with chickens.

♦

No one knows where the name *chicken pox* comes from.

[The earliest record of the name *chicken pox* comes from a description by the English naturalist Robert Johnson in 1684:

> There is an other sort of Pustules, or Tubercles … which are without Inflammation or redness; and also without a Fever. Some call them Cristals, others Blisters, but Country people call them Swine-pox, Hen or Chicken-pox, &c.

Johnson's mention that the infection was also called 'swine-pox' apparently contradicts the widely-held theory that the name *chicken pox* refers to a resemblance of the disease's characteristic bumpy rash to the welts and blisters caused by nips and pecks from chickens. Likewise, the idea that *chicken* is being used here as an affectionate name for a young child (and thereby refers to a childhood affliction) seems equally unlikely, not least because young children are rarely affectionately referred to as 'swine'. Instead, the most likely idea is that the name is somehow intended to show that chicken pox was considered a relatively mild infection, especially compared to the much more dangerous *smallpox*; as Samuel Johnson explained in his dictionary, the name apparently derives 'from its being of no very great danger'. None of these theories is watertight, however, and the name remains something of a mystery.]

A man who is *hen-pecked* is ruled by his wife. A parent who is *chicken-pecked* is ruled by their child.

A *peck-swarm* is a large swarm of bees.

In Tudor England, *honey brake* was flattering or overly eloquent language, particularly intended to persuade or charm someone.

Amongst Second World War troops, a *sugar report* was a letter sent by a soldier's girlfriend or sweetheart to the front line.

In the aftermath of the Second World War, *fratting* was the name given to the friendly and collaborative interaction of Allied troops and local women in parts of occupied Germany.

◆

Torschlusspanik is the general fear that time is running out, or another name for a mid-life crisis. It literally means 'gate-shut panic' in German.

◆

Panic literally refers to the Greek god of the woods, Pan.

> [Pan was the lecherous goat-legged god of woodland and pasture in Ancient Greece. He was also the god of theatrical criticism (make of that what you will), but as the chief god of the wilderness Pan was blamed for the eerily disembodied noises heard in forests and other remote places that could unnerve even the most hardened of hunters and travellers. Eventually, the adjective *panic* came to refer to any feeling of unease or anxiousness.]

◆

In naval history, a *panic party* was a group of extraneous crewmembers who would feign an evacuation from a ship in order to trick the enemy into thinking it was deserted.

◆

Crew cuts are named after the shorthaired crewmembers of America's Ivy League rowing teams.

◆

To pull your weight originally referred to rowers in a rowing team putting in enough effort in proportion to their own weight.

◆

A *kezayis* is a kosher unit of weight equal to the volume of one olive – reckoned to be around 35 ml.

◆

Oliver derives from an old Germanic name, Alfihar, literally means 'elf-host'.

◆

To give Roland for Oliver means 'to give as good as you get'.

[Roland was one of the nephews of the Holy Roman Emperor Charlemagne, who became the eponymous hero of a mediaeval French epic poem, *La Chanson de Roland* ('The Song of Roland'), in the eleventh century. Oliver was Roland's friend and counterpart, exactly equal to him in strength and fortitude, and together the pair were considered an unbeatable combination:

England all Olivers and Rolands bred
During the time Edward the Third did reign.
— *Henry VI* (I.ii), William Shakespeare

Some accounts of the story of Roland and Oliver suggest that the pair were originally adversaries, who met in combat on an island in the Rhine and were so identically matched that they fought solidly for days with no resolution; hence *to give a Roland for an Oliver* came to mean 'tit for tat' or 'to replace one thing for another' in the 1500s.]

♦

In the Middle Ages, saying that something has gone *oliver current* **meant that it had gone smoothly, or entirely according to plan.**

[*Oliver current* was borrowed into English from French in the early Middle Ages, but it's ultimately derived from the Latin equivalent *olivero currente*, which literally means 'with the olives running'. The allusion to something running 'without impediment' or 'without fault' is probably to an olive press, crushing a crop of olives to release a steady and smooth flow of oil.]

♦

The 'ZIP' of American *ZIP codes* **stands for 'Zone Improvement Plan'.**

♦

Zippers **were originally rubber boots that were fastened with a zip.** *Zips* **were originally called 'hookless fasteners'.**

♦

Gadzooks **is a contraction of 'God's hooks'.**

[*Gadzooks* is a seventeenth-century example of a 'minced oath', a euphemistic corruption of a more indelicate expletive – which in this case is 'God's hooks', the nails used to hold Jesus on the cross. So when an imprisoned painter is faced with the prospect of being castrated and 'reduced to the neuter gender' in Tobias Smollett's novel *The Adventures of Peregrine Pickle* (1751), he is well within his rights to respond:

> 'What! ... become a singer? Gadzooks! and the devil and all that! I'll rather be still where I am, and let myself be devoured by vermin.'

Gadzookery, meanwhile, is the deliberate use (and often overuse) of archaic language in modern historical literature; or, as one *New York Times* reviewer once defined it, 'the stumbling about of characters uttering quaint tidbits in a painted environment'.]

♦

Playing hookey is thought to derive from *hoekje spleen*, an old Dutch name for hide-and-seek.

[*Playing hookey* first appeared in a New York *Dictionary of Americanisms* in 1848, which supports the theory that it originated amongst Dutch settlers in America in the early nineteenth century before spreading elsewhere; it had reached British English, it seems, by the early 1920s when the quintessentially British writer P. G. Wodehouse used it in *The Inimitable Jeeves* (1923):

> He's got the shakiest reputation of any kid in the village. His name is as near to being mud as it can jolly well stick. He's played hookey from the choir so often that the vicar has told him, if one more thing happened, he would fire him out.

If not derived from Dutch, *hookey* might instead have something to do with the old nineteenth-century expression *hooky-crooky*, which meant simply 'crooked' or 'underhand', or else could be somehow related to *by hook or by crook*, in the sense of 'in any way possible', or 'regardless of the consequences'.]

♦

In Old English, a *hide* was the amount of land one family needed to support themselves – roughly defined as 120 acres, or the amount of land that could be ploughed in one year.

♦

In Ancient Greece, a *stremma* was a unit of area equal to the amount of land a person was able to plough in a day – around 1,000 square metres.

♦

A shape with 1,000 sides is called a *chiliagon* or *chiliahedron*.

> [The name *chiliagon* comes from the Greek word for 'thousand', *chilioi*, which is also the root of *chiliad* (a millennium, or a group of 1,000 things) and *chiliasm* (a religious philosophy based around cycles of 1,000 years). In practice, it's little more than a theoretical shape because unless a shape is enormously vast, as the number of its sides increases the less individually discernable they become. A chiliagon drawn on a piece of paper, for instance, would have to fit nearly three of its thousand sides into each degree of an equivalently-sized circle.]

♦

Around three-quarters of all written English is made up of the same thousand words.

♦

The ten words *the, and, I, to, of, a, you, my, in* and *that* account for a fifth of everything William Shakespeare wrote.

[Depending on what plays and editions are included, *The Complete Works of William Shakespeare* contains somewhere in the region of 885,000 words, of which his ten most frequently used words (those listed above) account for around 179,500, or just over 20 per cent. His 100 commonest words, meanwhile, account for around half of all of his writing.]

◆

In the seventeenth century, a *Fifth Monarchy-man* was someone who believed that the Second Coming of Christ was imminent and that the world would end in 1666.

[In the Old Testament, the prophet Daniel interprets a series of dreams told to him by the Babylonian king Nebuchadnezzar as fore-telling the rise and fall of four great kingdoms, the first of which is Nebuchadnezzar's own Babylonian Empire. Although scholars were long divided over the importance of Daniel's predictions, in the mid-1600s these verses inspired the rise of a radical Christian sect that believed that Daniel's 'four kingdoms' – identified as the Babylonian, Persian, Macedonian and Roman Empires – had all now come and gone, and that a fifth and final kingdom – namely the Second Coming of Jesus and the onset of the Apocalypse – must be imminent. The cult of these so-called *monarchy-men* rumbled on until 1661, when per-haps as many as 500 Fifth Monarchist rebels, led by a local barrel-maker named Thomas Venner, attempted to overthrow Oliver Cromwell and take the city of London in the name of Jesus Christ. Venner's Rising, as it became known, lasted for several days until the rebels were caught, charged with high treason, and executed; Venner's execution, 'with two more Fifth Monarchy men', is recorded in Samuel Pepys' diary on 19 January 1661.]

◆

Hexakosioihexekontahexaphobia is a fear of the number 666.

◆

A *Schnapszahl* or *repdigit* is a number comprised of a string of identical digits.

◆

The Thai equivalent of *LOL* is '555'.

> [The Thai word for 'five' is *hâa*, and so three of them in a row are pronounced 'ha-ha-ha'. Incidentally, in Mandarin 'five' is *wŭ*, and so '555' is used to represent the sound of crying.]

◆

Bangkok has the longest full name of any capital city in the world: *Krungthepmahanakhon Amonrattanakosin Mahintharayutthaya Mahadilokphop Noppharatratchathaniburirom Udomratchaniwetmahasathan Amonphimanawatansathit Sakkathattiyawitsanukamprasit.*

> [Bangkok's full ceremonial name contains 169 letters, although for ease it's usually abbreviated to *Krung Thep*, or 'the city of angels'. As well as being the world's longest capital city, it's also probably the world's longest place name, easily beating off competition from *Taumatawhaka tangihangakoauauotamateaturipukakapikimaungahoronukupokaiwhenuak itanatahu*, the eighty-five-letter Maori name of a hill on New Zealand's North Island, and Wales' fifty-eight-letter *Llanfairpwllgwyngyll gogerychwyrndrobwllllantysiliogogogoch*. America's longest place name is *Chargoggagoggmanchauggagoggchaubunagungamaugg*, the name of a lake in Massachusetts, which in comparison runs to a relatively tame forty-five letters.]

◆

Dysart, Dudley, Harcourt, Guilford, Harburn, Bruton, Havelock, Eyre and Clyde is the single name of a municipality in Ontario, Canada.

> [The United Townships of Dysart, Guilford, Dudley and Harburn came into being as a single settlement on 7 January 1867. Soon these four United Townships had grown large enough to subsume five more neighbouring townships around them – Harcourt, Bruton, Havelock, Eyre and Clyde – each of which in turn was added to the area's already lengthy full official name. It now stands at 'The Corporation of the United Townships of Dysart, Dudley, Harcourt, Guilford, Harburn, Bruton, Havelock, Eyre and Clyde' – although, for brevity, it is usually shortened to 'Dysart et al'.]

♦

The longest place name in Australia, *Mamungkukumpurangkuntjunya Hill*, means 'place where the devil urinates'.

♦

A *sydharb* is a unit of volume equal to 500,000 megalitres – the volume of Sydney Harbour.

> [It might seem like a fairly arbitrary measurement ('my car does 2.75 million miles to the sydharb' isn't a particularly useful comparison, after all) but the approximate size of Sydney Harbour is nevertheless used in a range of different circumstances in Australia to give much-needed context to otherwise unfathomably vast quantities, such as the capacity of reservoirs and lakes, the size of floods and other similar natural disasters, and figures of water use or storage. Australia's annual national water use, for instance, is an estimated fifty sydharbs.]

♦

A headland in Sydney, Australia is called *Tom Ugly's Point*.

◆

A *plug-ugly* was originally a criminal or gang member. No one knows what the 'plug' means.

◆

Uglyography is poor spelling.

◆

The 'bee' of *spelling-bee* is an eighteenth-century term for a meeting or 'coming together', alluding to the social cooperation of bees in a hive.

◆

The individual hexagonal compartments in a honeycomb are called *bee-cells*.

◆

A *Peter* is a nineteenth-century nickname for a prison cell, thought to be a reference to St Peter holding the keys to Heaven.

◆

A *peterman* is a thief who steals luggage from vehicles.

> [Based on the traditional image of St Peter holding the keys to the gates
> of Heaven, the name *Peter* has long been used of a number of similarly
> lockable and securable items in English criminal slang. Earliest of all
> of these was as a nickname for a suitcase or portmanteau, which dates
> back to the seventeenth century: a 'little canting vocabulary' outlined

in *The English Rogue* (1667), a 'Compleat History of the most Eminent Cheats of Both Sexes', explained that *to bite the Peter* meant to steal a suitcase (while *to heave a booth* meant to rob a house, *to pike on the leen* meant to run as fast as possible, and *to couch a hogshead* meant to go to sleep). By the early nineteenth century, *Peter* was also being used of safes or cashboxes, hence a *peterman* was a safebreaker in Victorian English, and by the early 1900s a *Peter* was a police lock-up or prison cell in Australian slang.]

♦

Samuel Johnson defined *luggage* as 'any thing of more weight than value'.

♦

***Valueless* originally meant 'invaluable'.**

♦

Anything *perquisquilian* or *skilligalee* is utterly worthless or trivially unimportant.

♦

The mediaeval saying *to pipe in with an ivy-leaf* means 'to entertain or console yourself with some trivial pastime'.

♦

***Hobbies* derive from *hobby horses*.**

[*Hobby* vs. *hobby horse* is another etymological chicken-and-the-egg problem, and just like *orange* vs. *oranges* the solution here isn't as obvious as it might seem. The earliest use of *hobby* in English is as the name of a small horse or pony, which dates from the early 1400s. From this came the first *hobby horses*, which were originally wooden or straw effigies of horses used in morris dances and other traditional performances, before the hobby horse as we know it today – a child's toy comprising a wooden horse's head on the end of a pole – emerged in the Tudor period.

By the late seventeenth century, people had begun referring to their pastimes as *hobby-horses*, implying that their hobby gives them as much pleasure as a hobby-horse gives a child – as the poet Sir Matthew Hale wrote in 1676, 'Almost every person hath some hobby horse or other wherein he prides himself'. This use of *hobby-horse* was shortened back to *hobby* in the early 1800s, and is the same *hobby* we use today to mean a casual interest or pastime.]

♦

A *road apple* is a lump of horse dung in the middle of a road.

♦

As a verb, *to apple* means 'to gather pinecones'.

[Confusingly, *pinecones* were originally known as *pine-apples* in English, and hence in the eighteenth century poorer families would often go *appling* – collecting pinecones to use as a free alternative to coal, because they tended to burn slowly while giving off a relatively large quantity of heat and light. *Pineapples*, meanwhile, were named after their resemblance to pinecones when they were first imported from the New World in the sixteenth century. Confusing things even more, pinecones were also once called *pine-nuts* – as well as *chats*, *clogs* and *fir-bobs*.]

♦

Pine martens were once called *sweet-marts* to differentiate them from polecats, which were called *foul-marts*.

♦

The word *foul-mouthed* was coined by Shakespeare.

♦

A *mushmouthed* person has a drawling, indistinct accent.

♦

No one knows why the Irish accent is called a *brogue*.

[A *brogue* was a type of shoe for two centuries before it began to be used of a pronounced Irish accent in the early 1700s, as in this essay, *On Barbarous Denominations in Ireland* (1728), by Jonathan Swift:

It is likewise true, that there is an odd provincial cant in most counties in England, sometimes not very pleasing to the ear; and the Scotch cadence, as well as expression, are offensive enough. But none of these defects derive contempt to the speaker: whereas, what we call the *Irish brogue* is no sooner discovered than it makes the deliverer in the last degree ridiculous and despised[.]

It's worth pointing out that at the time of writing Swift was Dean of St Patrick's Cathedral in Dublin, and his apparent dislike for the Irish accent seems to be partly prompted by his frustration over the inde-cipherable spellings of Irish place names, which he wished 'were a little better suited to the English mouth, if it were only for the sake of English lawyers; who, in trials upon appeals to the House of Lords, find so much difficulty in repeating the names, that, if the plaintiff or defendant were by, they would never be able to discover their own lands'.

Swift's opinions aside, quite how the Irish accent came to be known as a *brogue* is unclear. The most plausible explanation is that the two meanings are related, perhaps in the sense that Irish speakers would often wear brogues, or were known for their use of the word 'brogue' rather than 'shoe'. Alternatively, it could just as plausibly be a metaphor, implying a particularly weighty or noticeable accent, or the two words could be entirely unrelated, and instead an Irish *brogue* may actually be an Irish *barróg*, or 'an embrace'.]

♦

The Irish word for Christmas, *Nollaig*, is derived from *natalicius*, the Latin word for a birthday party.

♦

A *yule-hole* is the hole at the furthest end of a belt, to which it has to be fastened after overindulging at Christmas.

♦

In old English slang, a *C-and-E man* is someone who only attends church at Christmas and Easter.

♦

The first Sunday after Easter Sunday is called Quasimodo Day.

[The name *Quasimodo* is taken from the opening line of a Latin prayer, *quasi modo geniti infantes* ('as new-born babes'), which was once traditionally recited in church on the Sunday following Easter. In British English, this Sunday is usually known as Low Sunday (in the sense of a return to conventional church services after the previous week's festivities), but the alternative name 'Quasimodo Sunday' has been in occasional use ever since it was adopted from French in the early 1600s.

To most modern English speakers, however, the name Quasimodo is inextricably linked with Victor Hugo's *Notre-Dame de Paris* (1831) – according to the story, Hugo's tragic hunchback Quasimodo acquired his name when he was abandoned as a baby on the steps of Notre Dame Cathedral on Quasimodo Sunday.]

♦

In surfing, a *quasimodo* is a position in which the surfer stands at the front of the board with his head held down and his back hunched.

♦

The spray of water and surf blown across the surface of the sea by the wind is called *spindrift*.

♦

To spin street-thread once meant 'to spread gossip'.

♦

Gossip derives from the Old English word for 'godparent'.

♦

Gaffer, *compère* and *compadre* all mean 'godfather'.

♦

A *patroclinous* person resembles their father more than their mother. A *matroclinous* person resembles their mother more than their father.

♦

'If my uncle shaves your uncle, your uncle will be shaved' – *si mon tonton tond ton tonton, ton tonton sera tondu* – is a French tongue-twister.

◆

Your parents' male first cousins are your *Welsh uncles*.

◆

The Welsh word for 'carrots' is *moron*.

◆

A *moron* is specifically someone with an IQ of between 51–70.

> [At a meeting of the American Association for the Study of the Feeble-Minded in 1910, a psychologist named Henry H. Goddard proposed the adoption of three new intelligence classifications: *idiot*, used of someone with an IQ of 25 or less; *imbecile*, describing those whose IQ is between 26–50; and *moron*, the Greek word for 'stupid' or 'dull', which should describe anyone with an IQ of between 51–70 (or a mental age of between eight and twelve) and who, under Goddard's terms, 'is deficient in judgment [*sic*] or sense'. His definitions might sound bizarre to modern minds, but they remained the standard psychological classifications of intelligence for several decades until their association with the controversial eugenics movement in the 1920s and 30s, as well as their increasingly generalised use as insults in English, led them to be discarded.]

◆

Oxymoron derives from the Greek words for 'sharp' and 'dull'.

A *contronym* is a word that can be its own opposite – so 'dust' can mean both 'to remove dust', and 'to cover with powder'.

> [Also known as *auto-anonyms* or *Janus words* (after the two-faced god of Roman mythology), *contronyms* are a scarce but intriguing group of words whose multiple meanings apparently contradict one another. In some cases, these contradictory senses are unintentional, and emerge when two etymologically unrelated words come to have identical spellings: *cleave*, for instance, can mean both 'to split' (in which case it is derived from the Old English word *cleofan*) and 'to adhere to' (in which case it is taken from the unrelated Old English word *clifian*).
>
> Alternatively, a word can appear to take on oppositional meanings simply by being applied in new ways and contexts as a language develops over time. *Dust* originally meant 'to be dusty', but by the mid-1500s it had begun to be used to mean both 'to make dusty', and 'to make less dusty'. Although both meanings are opposites they derive from the same root and, unlike *cleave*, are etymologically related.]

♦

Africa is thought to derive from the Phoenician word for 'dust'.

♦

The plural of *mganga*, an East African wiseman, is *waganga*.

♦

A group of wizards is called a *congeries*.

♦

Wizard is one of the longest symmetrically balanced words: its first and last (W, D), second and second last (I, R), and third and third last letters (Z, A) are all equidistant from the centre of the alphabet.

[Symmetrical balance is a rare alphabetical quirk exhibited by only a handful of English words whose letters, when thought of as a series of ordinal numbers leading up to the centre of the alphabet (A=1, Z=1, B=2, Y=2 …) form a symmetrical pattern. The six letters of *wizard* make it one of the longest symmetrical words in the language: W is the fourth from last letter of the alphabet, while D is the fourth from first; I is the ninth letter of the alphabet, and R is ninth from last; Z is the last letter, and A is the first. Altogether, this gives *wizard* a symmetrical form of (4 9 1 1 9 4). Another six-letter example, *hovels*, likewise forms the pattern (8 12 5 5 12 8.)]

◆

CHECKBOOK, the American spelling of 'chequebook', is the longest English word with a line of horizontal symmetry.

[Nine upper-case letters have horizontal symmetry (B, C, D, E, H, I, K, O, X), which can be assembled to produce several entirely symmetrical words like CHICK, ICEBOX, ECHOED, KICKED, CHECKED, DECIDED, DIOXIDE, EXCEEDED, BOOHOOED, BEDECKED, COOKBOOK, CODEBOOK and, longest of all, CHECKBOOK – although if proper nouns are permitted, Florida's ten-letter Lake OKEECHOBEE steals the title. Likewise, the eleven letters with vertical symmetry (A, H, I, M, O, T, U, V, W, X, Y) can be arranged to form words like MIAOW, VOMIT, OUTWIT, WHAMMO, TATTOO, TOMATO, MAMMOTH, WITHOUT, MAXIMUM and AUTOMATA – although in order to maintain their symmetry these would need to be written vertically, one on top of the other.]

♦

Sterling, as in 'pound sterling', is an old English word meaning 'little star'. It refers to a design once printed on English coinage.

♦

To *quomodocunquise* means 'to make money by whatever means possible'.

♦

In the eighteenth century, a *master of the wardrobe* was someone who had pawned their clothes to get money for drink.

♦

Wardrobe is another name for badger excrement.

♦

Dachshund means 'badger-dog' in German.

♦

Amongst nineteenth-century American criminals, the *badger game* was a method of extorting money from a victim by luring them into a compromising situation and then blackmailing them.

♦

The opposite of *blackmail* is *white rent*.

[The 'mail' of *blackmail* is an ancient English word, *mal*, variously used to mean 'rent', 'payment', or 'reparations'. *White rent*, or *silver mail* as it was also known, was simply a rental payment made by a tenant to a landowner in cash:

> For white Rent, which is a Duty payable yearly by every Tinner in the County of Devon, and antiently [*sic*] due, that is, of every Tinner 8d. which sum in the whole, collected from 424 Tinners in that County, amounted to the sum of 14l 2s 8d.
>
> — *The History of the Dutchy of Cornewall* (1630),
> Sir John Doddridge

White rent dates back to the mid-1400s and presumably inspired its opposite, *blackmail*, which dates from the early 1500s. Originally, *blackmail* was a tax or tribute imposed by gangs of Scottish plunderers on farmers and landowners in the Borderlands and northernmost counties of England. The plunderers granted immunity to those farmers who paid the fee, and agreed to leave their lands untouched; those that failed to pay, however, were fair game. Unsurprisingly the practice was illegal, and the earliest record of *blackmail* in this context comes from a record of a criminal trial in Edinburgh in 1530:

> May 18 – Adam Scot of Tuschelow, Convicted of … art and part of theftuously taking Black-maill from the Tenants of Eschescheill – BEHEADED.]

◆

A *white-drop* is a snowflake. A *white-shower* is a snowstorm. A *white-burial* is one held during a *white-shower*.

◆

Snow-bones are the lines of snow left by the sides of roads and paths once the rest of the snow has melted.

♦

The Roman name for Ireland, *Hibernia*, is said to mean 'land of winters'.

♦

A *flattybouch* is someone who travels around by car in the summer, but returns home in the winter.

♦

A *Wanderjahr* is a year of constant travelling and sightseeing.

♦

A *wandering name* is a term that can be applied to various different things, or a word with several different meanings.

♦

The word *run* has 645 meanings in the *Oxford English Dictionary*.

♦

Drapetomania is an overwhelming urge to run away.

> [Derived from *drapetes*, the Greek word for a runaway slave, *drapeto-mania* was coined by a nineteenth-century American physician named Samuel Cartwright, who, as unpalatable as it seems today, defined it as a 'disease of the mind' that accounted for the otherwise inexplicable

desire for slaves to attempt to escape their captors. He based his theory on what he saw as 'the power which God has given [the white man] over his fellow man', and wrote in a medical journal in 1851 that in order to 'cure and prevent' *drapetomania*, slaves should be kept in 'that submissive state which it was intended for them to occupy'.

Twelve years later, on 1 January 1863, the Emancipation Proclamation was issued, and over the following years Cartwright's ideas were discredited and dropped into the realm of pseudoscience. Although the word itself has never been common, the meaning of *drapetomania* has steadily weakened over time and today, on the rare occasions that it is used in print, it tends only to imply a general desire to escape or to shirk one's responsibilities. If ever a word were a product of its time, *drapetomania* is it.]

♦

A *running mate* was originally a horse put into a race alongside a stronger one from the same stables in order to set its pace.

♦

A *dashboard* was originally a wooden screen that protected the driver of a horse-drawn carriage from being 'dashed' with mud.

♦

The earliest record of the phrase *'stick in the mud'* in English is as the nickname of an eighteenth-century burglar.

[As far back as the fifteenth century, writers were using expressions like 'stick in the briers' and 'stick in the mire' to describe someone who either finds themselves in a hopeless situation, or who stubbornly chooses to remain there despite offers of assistance. *Stick in the mud* is presumably derived from older expressions like these, and first began to appear in the language in the early 1700s as a nickname for an old-fashioned or non-progressive person, or for someone who lacks initiative or enterprise. One or all of these characteristics was presumably true of George Fluster, a criminal whose appearance in court in 1733 was recorded in London's *General Evening Post* of 15–17 November that year:

> George Sutton was Yesterday before Justice De Veil, on suspicion of robbing Col. Des Romain's House at Paddington. The Colonel was in the Room with the Justice, and no sooner had Sutton entered the Room, but the Colonel said, that is the Man that first came and seized me with his drawn Sword in his Hand. The Justice committed him to Newgate. At the same time James Baker was before Justice De Veil for the same Fact. The Colonel could not swear to him, but the Justice committed him to the same Place with Sutton. George Fluster, *alias* Stick in the Mud, has made himself an Evidence, and impeached the above two Persons.]

♦

Rhabdosophy is gesturing with a stick to help convey a meaning.

♦

A *whangee* is a walking stick made from bamboo.

♦

Bamboozle is thought to derive from *embabouiner*, a French word meaning 'to make a baboon of someone'.

♦

A *monkey's wedding* is a period of simultaneous sunshine and rain.

◆

In Tudor England, *to be wedded to the Duke of Exeter's daughter* meant 'to be tortured on the rack'.

> [There is some disagreement over precisely which Duke of Exeter is being alluded to in this sixteenth-century expression, but the two likeliest contenders are either John Holland, the 2nd Duke of Exeter and a cousin of Henry V, or else his son Henry Holland, the 3rd Duke of Exeter and a brother-in-law of Edward IV and Richard III. Both dukes served for a short time as Constable of the Tower of London in the mid-1400s, during which time one (or perhaps both) of the men became well known for his ruthless employment of the Tower's rack.]

◆

Phalarism is the taking of pleasure from torture or cruelty.

◆

Meaning 'a disproportionately severe punishment', the Russian equivalent of 'breaking a butterfly on the wheel' – *strelyat' iz pushek po vorob'yam* – means 'to shoot at sparrows with a cannon'.

◆

In the 1920s and 30s, a *butterfly man* was someone who paid with bad cheques.

◆

The Yiddish word for 'butterfly', *zomerfeygele*, literally means 'summer bird'.

♦

In the nineteenth century, *bald-headed butter* was a portion of butter in which there were no hairs.

♦

Balderdash was originally the name of a drink containing a jumbled mixture of beers or other liquors.

[*Balderdash* has been used to mean 'nonsense' or 'senseless chatter' since the late 1600s, but in the decades before then it apparently referred to a blended concoction of liquids and liquors. There seems to have been little consensus as to what those liquids actually were, however: a seventeenth century *Dictionary of English and French* translated *balderdash* as simply a '*mélange ridicule*', but in *Drinke & Welcome* (1637), a contemporary account of 'drinks in use now in Great Brittaine and Ireland', *balderdash* is described as 'beere, by a mixture of wine', and in his play *The New Inn* (1631) Ben Jonson called it 'beer and butter-milk, blended together'. Confusing things even further, the Elizabethan writer Thomas Nashe made reference to a 'bubbly spume or barber's balderdash' as early as 1599, which has led some etymologists to suggest the word might in fact once have referred to the basinful of soapy water used to give someone a shave.]

♦

A *cuckoo-ale* is a drink enjoyed outdoors.

♦

The earliest use of the word *booze* dates from the fourteenth century.

[There's a popular myth that *boozing* takes its name from a nineteenth-century American distiller named Edmund G. Booz, who famously sold his whiskey in bottles shaped like log cabins. In 1840, the Whig Presidential candidate William Henry Harrison began circulating bottles of Booz's whiskey to the electorate, hammering home the message that he too had been born in a log cabin, while simultaneously reinforcing Booz's association with liquor. Although Booz certainly existed, the idea that his name is the origin of *boozing* is unfortunately as well-founded as William Henry Harrison's presidency was lengthy (he died thirty-one days after his inauguration in 1841). In fact, *booze* is a corruption of an ancient English word, *bouse*, which as well as meaning 'to drink' or 'swill', was also the name of a drinking vessel. It's unclear precisely which of these two senses is implied in the following lines from *Mon in þe mone* ('The Man in the Moon'), an English ballad dating from the early 1300s at least, but given the context it seems that this is in fact the earliest known record of *boozing*:

> Drynke to hym deorly of fol god bous,
> ant oure dame douse shal sitten hym by,
> When þat he is dronke ase a dreynt mous,
> Þenne we schule borewe þe wed ate bayly
> [*Drink to him dearly with full, good booze,*
> *And our sweetheart shall sit beside him.*
> *When the man is drunk as a drowned mouse*
> *Then we shall redeem his pledge from the bailiff.*]]

♦

Happy hour was originally a US naval term for a period when entertainment would be provided for the crew of a ship.

♦

The word *happy* is used three times more often in English than *sad*.

◆

Hilary means 'cheerful'. It's derived from the same Latin root as *hilarious*.

◆

A *ha-ha* is a sunken, walled ditch that forms a boundary to a park or garden without interrupting the view.

◆

A *ho-ho* is a mythical phoenix-like bird used as an emblem of courage in Japanese folklore.

◆

Phoenix, Arizona was once called *Pumpkinville*.

◆

Pumpkinification is the extravagant or unworthy praise of something.

[*Pumpkinification* is the literal English translation of *Apocolocyntosis*, the title of a notorious Roman satire by Seneca the Younger that ridiculed the Emperor Claudius after his death in 54 AD. Seneca's *Apocolosyntosis* (a pun on *apotheosis*, the glorification of someone after their death) recounts Claudius's demise, his funeral procession, his ascent into Heaven, his damning judgement in front of the gods, and his ultimate descent into Hades where he is punished by having to perpetually search for dropped dice on the floor (a slight at the Emperor's love of gambling). Along the way, Seneca takes every chance he can to mock

Claudius, recalling and poking fun at his arrogance, his vindictiveness, his awkwardness and his disastrous leadership:

> The last words he was heard to speak in this world were these: when he had made a great noise with that end of him which talked easiest, he cried out, 'Oh dear, oh dear! I think I have made a mess of myself.' Whether he did or no, I cannot say, but certain it is he always did make a mess of everything.]

♦

Pumpernickel means 'farting goblin'.

♦

In the eighteenth century, a *catch-fart* was a footman or gentleman's assistant, so-called as he would walk directly behind his master.

♦

Feisty derives from an old English word for a flatulent dog.

[In a great bilingual glossary of Latin and Anglo-Saxon words written at the turn of the tenth century, Ælfric of Eynsham included two words – *feorting* and *fisting* – both of which meant 'to break wind'. Quite what Ælfric considered the distinction between the two is unknown (and probably best left that way), but while *feorting* eventually became *farting* in modern English, *fisting* gave rise to a handful of seemingly innocent words including *fizzle*, *foist* and *feisty*.

Derivatives like *fyst* or *fise* have been used since the early 1400s of anything that produced a bad smell ('a small windy escape backwards, more obvious to the nose than the ears', as the lexicographer Francis Grose defined a *foyse* in 1785), but several Tudor-period texts make references to 'foisting hounds', or 'fysting curs' – namely ladies' lapdogs that broke wind at the most inopportune times:

Canis Meliteus [an ancestor of the Maltese] ... This puppitly and pleasantly curre, (which some frumpingly tearme fysteing hounds), serve in a manner to no good vse except ... to succour and strengthen quailing and quammning stomackes to bewray bawdery, and filthy abbominable leudnesse.

— *Of English Dogges* (1576), John Caius

Besides being able to quell 'filthy abominable lewdness', these 'fysteing hounds' were also characteristically snappy and defensive, and it was this 'feistiness' that eventually gave rise to the word *feisty* as we know it today in the mid-nineteenth century.]

♦

A *fog-dog* is a clear spot or ray of light that breaks through a fog. A *rain dog* is a tiny portion of a rainbow, the rest of which is invisible. A *mist-bow* is an arc of white light that emerges as sunlight burns through mist.

♦

An inverted rainbow, caused by the refraction of sunlight through horizontal ice crystals in the sky, is called a *circumzenithal arc*.

♦

The Romanian word for 'rainbow', *curcubeu*, is derived from a Latin phrase meaning 'the ring that drinks'.

♦

Counting the rings on the inside of a tree in order to find out its age is called *dendrochronology*.

♦

Dendranthopology is the theory that mankind evolved from trees.

♦

Platygaeanism is the belief that the world is flat or disc-shaped.

♦

Eidolism is the proper name for believing in ghosts.

♦

A *phantomnation* is the image or illusion of a ghost.

> [Spookily enough, *phantomnation* itself is a 'ghost word' originating in a 1725 translation of Homer's *Odyssey* by Alexander Pope. Pope's original line read, 'Those solemn vows and holy offerings paid / To all the phantom-nations of the dead', but when 'phantom-nation' appeared in a supplement to Samuel Johnson's dictionary in 1820, the hyphen was omitted and the resulting word, *phantomnation*, was misguidedly given the definition, 'a multitude of spectres'. In the decades that followed this error was copied into and reinterpreted by several other dictionaries, including an 1864 edition of Webster's *American Dictionary of the English Language* that even credited the word to Pope, defining it as an 'appearance as of a phantom'.]

♦

A *ghost word* is one that shouldn't exist, but comes into existence due to an editorial blunder or spelling error.

♦

A *nihilartikel* or *Mountweazel* is a fictitious entry inserted into a dictionary or encyclopedia to prevent plagiarism.

[One of the earliest and most famous ghost words was *dord*, an imposter that found its way into the 1934 edition of *Webster's New International Dictionary* when an alphabet card for the letter D (reading 'D or d') was mistakenly filed amongst the entry words themselves. When the editors found that *dord* had inadvertently served to protect their work from plagiarism, many later dictionaries and encyclopaedias followed suit and began deliberately concealing invented entries, or *nihilartikels* (literally 'nothing-articles'), among their pages.

The 1975 *New Columbia Encyclopedia* included a whole fictitious biography for a 'Lillian Virginia Mountweazel', described as a 'fountain designer turned photographer', known for her images of rural American mailboxes. Her name has since become another byword for fake dictionary entries, thanks to the popularity of a 2005 article in *The New Yorker* that sought to uncover a fake word or 'Mountweazel' that the editors of the *New Oxford American Dictionary* had included in their second edition. After some etymological detective work, the bogus word was eventually found to be *esquivalience*, defined as 'the wilful avoidance of one's responsibilities'.]

♦

Nihil is the Latin word for 'nothing'. *Annihilate* literally means 'to reduce to nothing'.

♦

Absolute zero, the lowest theoretical temperature, was once also called 'infinite cold'.

♦

Curglaff is the uncomfortable shock of getting into cold water.

♦

In nineteenth-century naval slang, *to give cold pig* meant 'to wake someone up by pulling away their bedclothes and throwing cold water over them'.

♦

A *waterbed* was originally a bed on board a ship.

> [When the English poet and traveller George Sandys wrote in his travelogue *The Relation of a Journey* that he 'was forced to return to my water-bed' in 1615, we can be fairly sure he wasn't talking about a plastic water-filled mattress. In fact, despite sounding like the punchline to a terrible pun, when it first appeared in the language in the early seventeenth century a *waterbed* (and a *seabed* for that matter) was literally a bed 'on the water' – or in other words, a bed on board a ship. The first reference to an actual waterbed, incidentally, dates from 1844.]

♦

Waterloo means 'wet forest'.

♦

Soldiers of Napoleon's Old Guard Grenadiers were known as *grognards*, or 'grumblers'. It's now used of gamers who prefer out-dated versions of games to their newer equivalents.

♦

Ludicrous literally means 'playing a game'. It's derived from the same root as *ludo*.

♦

In German slang, a *Kiebitz* – literally a 'lapwing' – is someone who watches a game of cards but constantly interrupts with pointless comments and advice.

♦

A *lapwing stratagem* is any ploy intended to trick someone into missing or avoiding something you want to remain secret.

> [Lapwings nest on the ground, making their eggs and hatchlings easy prey for carnivorous creatures like foxes and stoats, and so with little else to protect them the adult birds are well known for adapting an extraordinarily wily strategy if they feel their nest is threatened. They pretend to be injured, holding one of their wings limp or even dragging it along the ground, and run in the opposite direction to the nest, thereby luring any potential predator away. This remarkably cunning tactic is the origin not only of the *lapwing stratagem* but also the bird's name, which is a compound of the Old English words for 'leap', *hleapan*, and 'totter' or 'stumble', *winc.*]

♦

Lapwings are also known as *tewits*, *peewits*, *peesweeps* and *teeacks*, all of which are supposed to emulate their call.

♦

A group of lapwings is called a *desert*.

♦

A crescent-shaped desert sand dune is called a *barchan*.

♦

In Victorian slang, a *sandillion* was an incalculably large number, equivalent to the number of grains of sand on a beach.

◆

A *sandgroper* is an inhabitant of Western Australia.

◆

Hanyauka means 'to tiptoe across hot sand' in the Kwangali Bantu language of Namibia.

◆

Anyone described as *tiptoe-nice* is overly and fastidiously prim and delicate.

◆

The *toe* of 'mistletoe' is derived from the Old English word for 'twig'.

◆

A *brancher* is a young bird that has just left the nest and begun hopping about the branches.

◆

A *bower-bird* is someone who collects useless but showy ornaments and trinkets.

◆

Knick-knacks are kept in a *knick-knackatory*.

◆

The *paddywhack* in the nursery rhyme *Knick Knack Paddy Whack*, or *This Old Man*, is a Victorian slang word for a severe beating.

◆

Silent letters – like the K of 'knock' or the B of 'doubt' – are properly known as *aphthongs*.

◆

Forecastle, the foremost part of the upper deck of a ship, is said to have more silent letters than any other English word.

> [The question of which English word has the most silent letters is a notoriously tricky one that depends largely on what is considered a 'silent' letter – the Ks of *knock*, *knee* and *knife* are silent, but what about the second E of *knee*, or the final E of *knife*? They too aren't pronounced, but without them ('ne' and 'nif') these words are unlikely to be pronounced correctly.
>
> Leaving all debate aside, *forecastle* is usually claimed to have the most silent letters of all English words, thanks to its popular pronunciation 'folk-sill'. This reduced form is often also found in print, as in Robert Louis Stevenson's *Treasure Island* (1883):
>
>> There was a great rush of feet across the deck. I could hear people tumbling up from the cabin and the fo'c's'le, and slipping in an instant outside my barrel, I dived behind the fore-sail, made a double towards the stern, and came out upon the open deck]

◆

A *forecastle-joke* is a crude practical joke, particularly one played on a new recruit or an inexperienced member of staff.

♦

Witzelsucht is a rare psychological condition whose sufferers have an uncontrollable urge to tell inappropriate jokes and stories.

> [*Witzelsucht* was first identified in 1889 by the German neurologist Herman Oppenheim, who coined the term from the German words for 'joke', *Witzel*, and 'yearning' or 'desire', *sucht*. Oppenheim had observed this peculiar phenomenon in four of his patients who, he later discovered, had all been suffering from tumours in the right frontal lobes of their brains. Although later cases were found to be caused by trauma to other parts of the brain, Oppenheim believed damage to the frontal lobe to be the primary cause of *Witzelsucht*, not least due to its role in recognising and predicting the consequences of situations, choosing between the best and worst courses of action, and both determining and suppressing unacceptable responses.]

♦

The earliest record of a *knock-knock joke* dates from 1934.

> [*Knock-knock* jokes developed from a nineteenth-century children's game called 'Buff', which employed a circuitous back-and-forth dialogue between two players: 'Knock, knock!'; 'Who's there?'; 'Buff!'; 'What says Buff?'; 'Buff says Buff to all his men, and I say Buff to you again.' Different versions of the game continued this dialogue with ever more ludicrous lines and verses, the aim of all of which was to make 'Buff' laugh. If it worked, he would pay a forfeit and then the game would start again.
>
> By the early 1900s, this verbal back-and-forth had begun to develop

into the first knock-knock jokes, the earliest of which appeared in print in a local newspaper in Iowa, *The Rolfe Arrow*, on 10 September 1934:

> Knock—Knock.
> Who's there?
> Rufus.
> Rufus who?
> Rufus the most important part of your house.

In 2010, another early example was discovered in a letter written by Jim Richardson, the steward of Edward VIII's luxury yacht the *Nahlin*, in 1936 – the same year as Edward's abdication. Writing home to his mother while he accompanied the king and Wallis Simpson on a Mediterranean cruise, Richardson reiterated a popular joke of the time: 'Knock knock. Who's there? Edward Rex. Edward Rex who? Edward wrecks the Coronation.' He also commented that the king was 'drinking heavily', and that Mrs Simpson was 'not good looking', with 'a very big mouth ... and a very high pitched metallic American voice'.]

♦

Kowtow literally means 'knock the head' in Chinese.

♦

The *bun* hairstyle takes its name from a French word, *buinge*, meaning 'a swelling caused by a blow to the head'.

♦

In the nineteenth century, a *swell mob* was a gang of criminals and pickpockets who dressed as respectable gentlemen in order to escape being detected.

[*Swell mobs* like these were also known as *flash mobs*. 171 years separate the earliest record of a criminal *flash mob* in an 1832 edition of *The Morning Chronicle*, and the first modern use of *flash mob* to refer to a

group of people who secretly meet for a prearranged public perform-
ance in 2003.]

♦

An *ochlagogue* is the leader or manipulator of a mob.

♦

A *mob* is a group of emus.

♦

Kurdaitcha are native Aboriginal shoes made from emu
feathers stuck together with human blood.

♦

A *blood and sand* is a cocktail containing Scotch whisky,
cherry brandy and vermouth mixed with blood orange
juice.

♦

Arena is derived from the Latin word for sand, *harena*,
as Roman amphitheatres would be dusted with sand to
soak up combatants' blood.

♦

Amphitheatre literally means 'viewing on both sides'.

♦

A book or document that is *opisthographic* has text
printed on both sides of the paper.

♦

Eucalyptus means 'well-covered' in Greek.

♦

Koalas were once known as *monkey-bears*.

♦

In Victorian slang, *to have a monkey up the chimney* meant 'to have mortgaged your house'.

♦

Mortgage derives from the French for 'death contract'.

♦

A *death assemblage* is the complete set of fossils collected from a single paleontological site.

♦

A *fossil word* is one that is only retained in the language in a handful of isolated phrases and contexts – like the *immemorial* of 'time immemorial'.

> [A number of English expressions contain 'fossilised' words, many of which are so familiar that they're used without a second thought to what the words themselves might mean. The *sleight* of 'sleight of hand', for instance, is an old word for skilfulness; the *batten* of 'batten down the hatches' is a seventeenth-century word for a piece of timber; and a *petard* was a rudimentary explosive often so poorly-made that it would detonate before being put in place – hence you could be 'hoist by your own petard', a phrase apparently coined by Shakespeare in *Hamlet* (III.iv):

For 'tis the sport to have the engineer
Hoist with his own petard; and't shall go hard
But I will delve one yard below their mines,
And blow them at the moon[.]]

♦

In legal parlance, *time immemorial* originally referred to any event occurring before 6 July 1189.

[*Time immemorial* literally means 'time beyond memory'. In 1275, the first ever Statute of Westminster standardised precisely what that meant by limiting the 'time of memory' to the reign of Richard I, beginning with his coronation on 6 July 1189. This definition remained in force in England until 1832, when *time immemorial* was redefined as 'time whereof the memory of Man runneth not to the contrary' – or between twenty and thirty years.]

♦

July was once known as *Afterlithe*, meaning 'later mild weather'.

♦

Sun-wake is the reflection of the sunset or sunrise on the surface of the sea.

♦

Claude Monet's 1872 painting *Impression, soleil levant* ('Impression, Sunrise') is the origin of the term *impressionism*.

[In 1874, a group of French painters including Monet, Renoir, Pisarro and Degas rejected the established art world, set up their own 'Anonymous Society of Painters, Sculptors, Engravers, &c.', and opened their own exhibition at 35 Boulevard des Capucines in Paris. In total, more than 160 paintings were exhibited, all of which employed a radical new art technique that seemed rough, hurried and unfinished to the public, and was lambasted by critics. In his review in *Le Charivari* newspaper, the writer Louis Leroy dismissed the whole exhibition as an *'exposition des impressionistes'*, apparently inspired by Monet's *Impression, soleil levant* – although he had meant the title to be insulting, Leroy instead gave the entire movement its name.]

♦

The expression *the usual suspects* comes from a line spoken by Claude Rains in *Casablanca*.

♦

Casablanca means 'white house'.

♦

In the nineteenth century, shoemakers were nicknamed *ambassadors of Morocco*.

♦

The *Atlantic Ocean* is named after the Atlas Mountains in Morocco.

♦

Ocean derives from *okeanos*, the name of a great river the Ancient Greeks believed encircled the Earth.

♦

An *epirot* is someone who lives nowhere near the coast.

♦

A *godsend* was a nickname for a shipwreck among people living along the coast.

♦

The Arabic equivalent of 'too many cooks spoil the broth' is 'too many captains sink the ship'.

♦

The magic word *shazam* first appeared in the *Captain Marvel* comic strip.

> [The earliest record of the word *shazam* comes from a 1940 edition of *Whiz Comics*, in which a young Billy Batson is transformed into Captain Marvel for the very first time. The acronymic magic word *shazam* ultimately grants Billy 'the wisdom of Solomon', 'the strength of Hercules', 'the stamina of Atlas', 'the power of Zeus', 'the courage of Achilles' and 'the speed of Mercury'.]

♦

In the eighteenth century, *captain-lieutenant* was a slang nickname for inferior quality beef.

> [This ingenious nickname presumably arose amongst the military, wherein a man holding the rank of captain-lieutenant has almost the same authority as a captain, but receives the poorer wage of a lieutenant. The implication here is that *captain-lieutenant* meat is too old to be still classed as veal, but too young to be good quality beef.]

♦

The *beefeaters* of the Tower of London are so-called because, as servants of the Royal Family, they would be very well fed.

◆

The earliest record of an animal being called a *man-eater* was an unknown species of shark in 1677.

◆

Hammerhead sharks were originally called *balance-fish*.

◆

Balance derives from *bilanx*, the Latin word for a scale with two pans.

◆

Something described as *equipondious* is precisely balanced so as to carry the same weight on both sides.

◆

An *ambidexter* is a lawyer who took pay from both the plaintiff and the defendant.

◆

A *sea lawyer* is a tiger shark. A *Penang lawyer* is a walking stick. A *bush lawyer* is a climbing blackberry.

◆

A *cunningberry* is a foolish or particularly gullible person.

◆

A *cunning-man* or *-woman* is a fortune-teller or astrologer.

◆

Machaeromancy is a form of divination that uses knives and blades.

♦

To *snickersnee* means 'to fight with knives'.

♦

Mumblety-peg was a Tudor game in which players attempted to throw knives into the ground, with the loser having to pull a peg out of the ground using their teeth.

♦

Winnipeg means 'dirty water'.

♦

To be *impluvious* means to be completely soaked with rain.

♦

A Roman *compluvium* was a hole in a roof through which rain would fall and be channelled away.

♦

The Bristol Channel was originally called the North Sea.

[What we know as the North Sea today was first referred to as such in an eighth-century East Anglian document, which described 'a fen of immense size' that 'extends to the North Sea, with numerous wide and lengthy meanderings'. Before then, the North Sea had been *Septentrionalis Oceanus*, or the great 'northern ocean', to the Romans; the ancient Celts had known it as *Morimarusa*, or 'the dead sea'; and until as relatively recently as the 1830s, it was still being labelled as the 'German Ocean' on maps and atlases.

Confusingly, the Bristol Channel was also once known as the North Sea, as in the following account from the *Anglo-Saxon Chronicle* of an invasion of a fleet of Danish ships in 893 AD:

> … sum feowertig scipa norþ ymbutan, ymbsæton an geweorc on Defnascire be þære norþsæ; þa þe suð ymbutan foron ymbsæton Exancester.
>
> [*some forty ships went north about, and besieged a fort in Devonshire by the north sea; and those who went south about beset Exeter.*]

In fact the Bristol Channel was still being referred to as 'the North Sea' as late as the seventeenth century, with the Tudor writer Richard Carew unfairly describing 'Bottreuax Castle' (the village of Boscastle in Cornwall) as standing 'on a bad harbour of the North sea, & suburbed with a poore market town'.]

♦

Bristol-stones are sham diamonds.

♦

In nineteenth-century criminals' slang, *to diamond a horn* meant to place a stone in your shoe in order to fake lameness.

♦

Knibblockie is an old Scots word for rough, stony path or road.

♦

The Rocky Mountains were once called 'The Stony Mountains'.

To be rocked in a stone cradle once meant 'to have been born in a prison'.

As a nickname for a prison, *clink* is thought to derive from The Clynck, a sixteenth-century jail in London.

London ivy is thick smog.

Smog is a combination of 'smoke' and 'fog'. *Vog* is 'volcanic smog'.

Vulcan was the name of a planet once believed to lie between Mercury and the Sun.

> [Astronomers in mid-nineteenth century France spent several decades searching for Vulcan – named after the fire-loving god of volcanoes and blacksmiths in Roman legend – under the mistaken belief that the gravitational pull of an undiscovered planet even closer to the Sun must be responsible for bizarre shifts that had been observed in Mercury's orbit. Despite several false alarms and claims of discoveries in the 1860s and 70s, the astronomers of course found nothing. And once Albert Einstein was finally able to explain Mercury's eccentric orbit in terms of his Theory of Relativity in 1915, the concept of a tiny unseen planet between Mercury and the Sun was finally abandoned.]

The consecutive chemical elements *uranium*, *neptunium* and *plutonium* are named after the consecutive planets Uranus, Neptune and Pluto.

♦

Plutomania is an obsession with or heedless pursuit of wealth.

♦

The earliest reference to money *burning a hole in your pocket* dates from 1529.

♦

A *pocket-tortoise* is another name for a comb.

♦

The Dutch word for 'tortoise', *schildpad*, means 'shield-toad'.

♦

A *toadstone* is a stone said to form in the heads of toads which has mysterious healing and protective powers.

♦

An *aetites* or 'eagle-stone' is a small hollow geode, once supposed to have various magical and medicinal properties.

[According to the Roman physician Dioscorides, as well as treating epilepsy, reversing the affects of poison, and even being able to discover thieves and other guilty parties, *aetites* stones could be used to promote fertility, protect expectant mothers, and encourage a safe birth. Another first-century Roman scholar, Pliny the Elder, claimed that *aetites* stones could only be obtained from eagles' nests, where they are always found in pairs, one each representing the male and female birds. Without them, he claims, the eagles 'would be unable to propagate'. The stones' ancient association with propagation and pregnancy stems from their composition: aetites are comprised of hydrated iron oxide, a mineral that forms a tough outer shell around a softer and often hollow core. Small shards of this softer material can break away and rattle around in the stone's centre – making the stones themselves appear 'pregnant'.]

♦

A group of eagles is called a *convocation*.

♦

The name *Arnold* literally means 'eagle-power'.

♦

Spread-eagleism is an excessive fondness or extravagant praise of the United States.

♦

The earliest recorded use of the name *America* dates from 1507.

♦

South America is the only continent with all five vowels in its name.

♦

Isthmi and *asthma* are two of the longest English words that begin and end with a vowel, but have no vowels in between.

> [Other English words with this particular quirk in common are much less familiar, but nevertheless include *aphtha*, an old name for a mouth ulcer; *eltchi*, a title once held by Turkish ambassadors; and *armthe*, an old word for poverty or misery. *Isthmi*, incidentally, is the plural of 'isthmus', a narrow strip of land connecting two larger landmasses, like the Panamanian isthmus connecting North and South America.]

♦

Panama hats originated in Ecuador.

♦

Ecuador is the Spanish word for 'equator'.

> [The Spanish-speaking Republic of Ecuador lies directly on the equator, sandwiched between Colombia and Peru, on the Pacific coast of South America. It is one of only two countries in the world named after any one of the lines of latitude or longitude that traverse the globe, the other being Africa's Equatorial Guinea – which doesn't actually lie on the equator, but rather straddles it.]

♦

The equator takes its name from the Latin *aequator diei et noctis*, meaning 'equalizer of day and night'.

♦

Anything described as *nuchthemerinal* lasts precisely one day and one night; a *nycthemeron* is a period of twenty-four hours.

♦

Attaint is an old legal process in which a jury of twenty-four *attaintors* could reverse the decision of a previous jury and have them convicted instead.

♦

A *jury-mast* is a temporary or makeshift mast on board a ship erected in place of one that has been damaged.

> [The prefix *jury-* has been used since the early 1600s to imply that something is ramshackle, or has been put together as a temporary replacement for something broken. A *jury-leg*, for instance, was once a wooden leg:
>
> > I took the leg off with my saw as well as any loblolly-boy in the land could have done – heated my broad axe, and seared the stump … and made a jury-leg that he shambles about with as well as ever he did.
> >
> > — *The Pirate* (1822), Sir Walter Scott
>
> *Jury* in this sense is presumably derived from 'injury', but another theory claims it is instead taken from the French word for 'day', *jour*, implying that a *jury-mast* or *jury-leg* might only be a temporary replacement.]

♦

The earliest use of the word *skyscraper* dates from 1794 as the name of a particularly tall mast on a ship.

♦

The first building called a *skyscraper* was built in Chicago.

[The world's first *skyscraper* was Chicago's Home Insurance Building completed in 1885. At 138 ft tall, it was able to reach its then unprecedented height thanks to a unique integrated metal framework, which became known as the 'Chicago skeleton'. This 'skeleton' was soon in use all across America (the Home Insurance Building was demolished in the same year that the nine-times-taller Empire State Building was completed), but Chicago's place in architectural history was assured: a local newspaper article declared that 'the "sky-scrapers" of Chicago outrival anything of their kind in the world' as early as 1888.]

♦

Chicago derives from a Native American word meaning 'wild onion'.

♦

Onion is derived from the Latin word for the number one.

♦

A *lipogram* is a piece of text that deliberately avoids using one particular letter, or letters, of the alphabet.

♦

A *telestich* is a poem or column of words whose final letters spell out a hidden message.

♦

The word *therein* contains nine more words inside it: *there, the, he, her, here, herein, ere, rein* and *in*.

[Crucially, the letters of the words listed here have not been rearranged – these aren't anagrams, but simply chains of consecutive letters that happen to spell out pre-existing words. For such a short word, the nine words found inside *therein* are probably a record – and can be stretched to twelve if words like *re* (the second note of the musical scale), *er* (to hesitate) and the single-letter pronoun *I* are added to the total.]

♦

Nine-killer is an old name for the shrike, a carnivorous bird supposedly known for killing its prey nine at a time.

♦

The spikes on the ends of an anchor are called *flukes*.

♦

A *prickle* is a group of porcupines.

♦

Porcupine means 'spiny-pig'.

♦

A *pig's whisper* is a proverbially short amount of time.

♦

Whisper-shot is the distance within which a whisper can be overheard.

[The *shot* here is the same as in more familiar words like *eyeshot* and *earshot*, and it's likely that *whisper-shot* was coined using one or both of these earlier words as a template in the late nineteenth century. Similarly, an *arm-shot* is the range of a person's reach.]

♦

A *secret de Polichinelle* is a 'stage whisper' – a line spoken only to the audience. It's also used of a secret that is actually known to everyone.

> [*Polichinelle* is the French name of Punchinello, a clownish stock character from the *commedia dell'arte* theatre that emerged in Europe in the seventeenth century. A *secret de Polichinelle* is his aside to the audience, a comment addressed to the audience that is intended not to be heard by the other characters onstage. As a comment broadcast to a group of people, however, Punchinello's *secret* has become a byword for really no secret at all – a piece of gossip or old news, a secret known to everyone.]

♦

Shibboleth, another name for a watchword or secret password, is the Hebrew word for 'ear of corn'.

> [According to the Old Testament, the Gileadites used the Hebrew word *shibboleth* to differentiate their own men from the opposing Ephraimites, because they couldn't pronounce the 'sh' sound properly:
>
> > … when those Ephraimites which were escaped said, Let me go over [the river Jordan]; that the men of Gilead said unto him, Art thou an Ephraimite? If he said, Nay; Then said they unto him, Say now 'Shibboleth': and he said 'Sibboleth': for he could not frame to pronounce it right. Then they took him, and slew him at the passages of Jordan[.]
> >
> > — Judges 12:5–6]

♦

A *nubbin* is a stunted or only partly grown ear of corn.

♦

A *nubbin-stretcher* is a heavy shower of rain.

♦

Stretching and yawning when tired or waking up is called *pandiculation*.

♦

The Dutch word for 'morning', *morgen*, is also the name for the area that can be ploughed by a team of cattle in one morning – anywhere between one half and two and a half acres.

♦

May was known as *þrimilce* in Old English, as it was traditionally the month when cattle could be milked three times a day.

♦

White meat was originally dairy produce.

♦

Album is derived from the Latin for 'white', and originally referred to a blank or unused stone tablet in Ancient Rome.

♦

A *tabloid* was originally a small tablet.

♦

A *feuilleton* – literally a 'little leaf' – is a newspaper column dedicated to general interest articles, literature and critiques.

♦

The part of a drawbridge that opens and closes is called the *leaf.*

♦

As well as describing a tree that sheds its leaves, the adjective *deciduous* can refer to any impermanent feature that is eventually discarded – like a child's milk teeth, or a deer's antlers.

♦

In German slang, an *evergreen* is an enduringly popular song or old standard.

♦

The American green heron is nicknamed the *shitepoke* because of its habit of defecating when it is disturbed or takes flight.

♦

Boterschijte, an old Dutch name for a butterfly, literally means 'butter-shitter'.

♦

Smörgåsbord means 'butter-goose-table' in Swedish.

◆

The earliest record of the phrase *to say boo to a goose* dates from 1588.

◆

The Czech word *vybafnout* means 'to frighten someone by jumping out and yelling "boo!"'

◆

Blutterbunged, stamagastered and *forglopned* all mean 'surprised' or 'shocked'.

◆

Aghast literally means 'frightened by a ghost'.

◆

A *psychomanteum* is an entirely mirrored room used to communicate with the dead.

◆

Catoptromancy is a form of fortune telling using mirrors and reflections.

◆

A *burning-glass* is a concave mirror or lens that concentrates sunlight to produce a combustible effect.

◆

A *glancing-glass* is a priest or minister whose extravagant showmanship outweighs his knowledge of the Bible.

♦

Inspired by circus impresario P. T. Barnum, to *barnumise* means 'to promote something with outlandish promises'.

♦

Shakespeare used the word *advertising* to mean 'paying attention to'.

♦

The word *impeticos* appears in *Twelfth Night*. No one knows for sure what it means.

[The *Oxford English Dictionary* describes *impeticos* as 'a burlesque word put into the mouth of a fool', and they're quite right – it appears in a line spoken by the clown, Feste, in *Twelfth Night* (II.iii), but what it actually means remains unclear, and it has troubled editors and directors for years. The full line reads, 'I did impeticos thy gratillity', which is usually taken to mean that Feste has 'impocketed' (in other words, 'kept') a 'gratuity' of sixpence, paid to him by the equally clownish Sir Andrew Aguecheek. Alternatively, *impeticos* could mean 'impetticoat', alluding either to the long cloaks worn by clowns and fools, or to the fact that Feste has already spent the cash on an unnamed woman.

This line even puzzled renowned Shakespearolater Samuel Johnson, who commented that 'There is yet much in this dialogue which I do not understand'. But it was the Victorian writer Alexander Dyce, author of a renowned nineteenth-century *General Glossary to Shakespeare's Works*, who complicated matters even further, by pointing out that 'When a boy at Aberdeen, I remember seeing a fullgrown man, an idiot, who wore a long petticoat, and was led about the streets, as an object of charity, by his mother'.]

◆

Petticoat means 'little coat'. It originally referred to a padded cloth coat worn under a suit of armour.

◆

An *armoury* is a group of aardvarks.

Select Bibliography

The basis for researching any book of this kind is of course the *Oxford English Dictionary*, which remains not only the finest English language dictionary ever compiled, but one of the greatest scholarly achievements of any kind. Given that sheer breadth of subjects and languages we have covered here, however, an array of other titles was also consulted, a full and complete list of which would undoubtedly span several increasingly monotonous pages. Instead, listed here are all those titles – both ancient and modern – that were consulted on more than one occasion during the development of this project, and without which this book would simply not have been possible. Anyone with an interest in words, word origins, or language history would find much to admire in any one of these titles, and they would make a worthy addition to any logophile's bookshelf.

Aldrich, Chris. *The Aldrich Dictionary of Phobias and Other Word Families*. Victoria, 2002.

Ayto, John. *Dictionary of Word Origins*. New York, 2001.

Ayto, John. *20th Century Words*. Oxford, 1999.

B. E. *A New Dictionary of the Terms Ancient and Modern of the Canting Crew*. London, c.1698.

Bailey, Nathaniel. *An Universal Etymological English Dictionary*. London, 1749.

Barnhart, Robert K. (Ed.) *Barnhart Dictionary of Etymology*. New York, 1988.

Barrère, Albert, and C. Leland. *A Dictionary of Slang, Jargon and Cant*. London, 1889.

Blount, Thomas. *Glossographia*. London, 1656.

Boswell, James. *The Life of Samuel Johnson*. London, 1791.

Brewer, E. Cobham. *Dictionary of Phrase and Fable*. Philadelphia, 1887.

Bullokar, John. *An English Expositor*. London, 1616.

Byrne, Josefa Heifetz. *Mrs Byrne's Dictionary of Unusual, Obscure and Preposterous Words* (Reprint Ed.) London, 1989.

Chambers, Robert. *The Book of Days: A Miscellany of Popular Antiquities*. London, 1864.

Clapin, Sylva. *A New Dictionary of Americanisms*. New York, 1902.

Cockeram, Henry. *The English Dictionary: An Interpreter of Hard English Words*. London, 1623.

Cotgrave, Randle. *A Dictionarie of the French and English Tongues*. London, 1611.

Coxe, Richard. *A Pronouncing Dictionary*. London, 1813.

Cresswell, Julia. *Oxford Dictionary of Word Origins* (2nd Ed.) Oxford, 2009.

Crystal, Ben, and David Crystal. *Shakespeare's Words: A Glossary and Language Companion*. London, 2004.

De Vere, Schele. *Americanisms: The English of the New World*. New York, 1871.

Donald, James. *Chambers's Etymological Dictionary of the English Language*. London, 1877.

Donkin, T. C. *An Etymological Dictionary of the Romance Languages*. Edinburgh, 1864.

Farmer, John S. *Slang and Its Analogues Past and Present*. London, 1890.

Farmer, John S. (Ed.) *The Proverbs, Epigrams and Miscellanies of John Heywood*. London, 1906.

Farmer, John S., and W. E. Henley. *A Dictionary of Slang and Colloquial English*. London, 1905.

Fraser, Edward, and John Gibbons. *Soldier and Sailor Words and Phrases*. London, 1925.

Freeman, Morton S. *A New Dictionary of Eponyms*. Oxford, 1997.

Gelling, Margaret. *Signposts to the Past: Place-Names and the History of England* (3rd Ed.) Chichester, 1997.

Goldin, Hyman E. *The Dictionary of American Underworld Lingo*. New York, 1950.

Grant, William. *The Scottish National Dictionary*. Edinburgh, 1931–41.

Green, Jonathan. *Chambers Slang Dictionary*. London, 2008.

Green, Jonathan. *Newspeak: A Dictionary of Jargon*. London, 1984.

Grose, Francis. *A Classical Dictionary of the Vulgar Tongue*. London, 1785.

Grose, Francis. *A Glossary of Provincial and Local Words Used in England*. *London*, 1787.

Halliwell, James. *A Dictionary of Archaic and Provincial Words*. London, 1855.

Harrison, Henry. *Surnames of the United Kingdom: A Concise Etymological Dictionary* (Reprint Ed.) Baltimore, 2013.

Heywood, John. *Proverbs in the English Tongue*. London, 1546.

Holloway, William. *A General Dictionary of Provincialisms*. London, 1840.

Hollyband, Claudius. *A Dictionary of French and English*. London, 1593.

Hotten, John Camden. *The Slang Dictionary*. London, 1887.

Jamieson, John. *An Etymological Dictionary of the Scottish Language*. Paisley, 1879.

Johnson, Samuel. *A Dictionary of the English Language*. London, 1755.

Jones, Stephen. *A General Pronouncing and Explanatory Dictionary*. London, 1818.

Kipfer, Barbara Ann (Ed.), and Robert L. Chapman. *Dictionary of American Slang* (4th Ed.) New York, 2007.

Klein, Ernest. *A Comprehensive Etymological Dictionary of the English Language*. Amsterdam, 1971.

Knowles, James. *A Pronouncing and Explanatory Dictionary of the English Language*. London, 1835.

Lehmann, Winfred P. *A Gothic Etymological Dictionary*. Leiden, 1986.

Liberman, Anatoly. *Analytic Dictionary of English Etymology*. Minneapolis, 2008.

Maclennan, Malcolm. *Gaelic Dictionary*. Edinburgh, 1925.

Manser, Martin H. *The Wordsworth Dictionary of Eponyms* (Reprint Ed.) Ware, 1996.

Marples, Morris. *University Slang*. London, 1950.

Mills, A. D. *A Dictionary of English Place Names* (2nd Ed.) Oxford, 1998.

Mollett, J. W. *An Illustrated Dictionary of Words Used in Art and Archaeology*. London, 1883.

Nares, Robert. *A Glossary or Collection of Words, Phrases, Names, and Allusions […] in the Works of English Authors, Particularly Shakespeare, and his Contemporaries*. London, 1859.

Onion, C. T. *A Shakespeare Glossary*. Oxford, 1911.

Partridge, Eric. *A Dictionary of Catchphrases* (2nd Ed.) London, 1985.

Partridge, Eric. *A Dictionary of Clichés*. London, 1940.

Partridge, Eric. *A Dictionary of Forces Slang, 1935–1945*. London, 1948.

Partridge, Eric. *A Dictionary of Slang and Unconventional English* (8th Ed.) London, 1984.

Partridge, Eric. *A Dictionary of the Underworld*. London, 1949.

Partridge, Eric. *The Routledge Dictionary of Historical Slang* (Revised 6th Ed.) London, 1973.

Pegler, Martin. *Soldiers' Songs and Slang of the Great War*. Oxford, 2014.

Pepys, Samuel. *The Diary of Samuel Pepys: A New and Complete Transcription* (Robert Latham and William Matthews, Eds.) London, 1970–83.

Phillips, Edward. *The New World of English Words*. London, 1658.

Reaney, Percy Hide, and Richard Middlewood Wilson. *A Dictionary of Surnames, Revised Edition*. Oxford, 1997.

Robertson, John G. *Robertson's Words for a Modern Age* (Reprint Ed.) London, 1991.

Robinson, C. Clough. *A Glossary of Words Pertaining to the Dialect of Mid-Yorkshire*. London, 1876.

Schneider, Lucien. *Ulirnaisigutiit: An Inuktitut-English Dictionary*. Laval, 1985.

Sheard, K. M. *Llewellyn's Complete Book of Names […] from Every Place and Every Time*. Woodbury, MN, 2011.

Sheridan, Thomas. *A Complete Dictionary of the English Language*. London, 1790.

Skeat, Walter. *A Glossary of Tudor and Stuart Words*. Oxford, 1914.

Smith, Alexander. *The Thieves' New Canting Dictionary*. London, 1719.

Smyth, William. *The Sailor's Word-Book: An Alphabetical Digest*. London, 1867.

Walker, John. *A Critical Pronouncing Dictionary and Expositor of the English Language*. Edinburgh, 1835.

Warrack, Alexander. *A Scots Dialectic Dictionary*. Edinburgh, 1911.

Watts, Victor. *The Cambridge Dictionary of English Place-Names*. Cambridge, 2004.

Webster, Noah. *A Compendious Dictionary of the English Language*. New Haven, 1806.

Wedgwood, Hensleigh. *A Dictionary of English Etymology*. New York, 1878.

Wentworth, Harold. *American Dialect Dictionary*. New York, 1944.

Wilkinson, P. R. *Wilkinson's Thesaurus of Traditional English Metaphors* (2nd Ed.) London, 2002.

Worcester, Joseph. *A Dictionary of the English Language*. Boston, 1881.

Wright, Joseph. *The English Dialect Dictionary (Vols. 1–6)*. Oxford, 1896–1905.

Wright, Thomas. *Dictionary of Obsolete and Provincial Words*. London, 1857.